THE MIRROR NEVER LIES

FROM REFLECTION TO PROSPERITY
– THE BLUEPRINT FOR
SUCCESS AND FULFILMENT

IVAN BARTOLO

Published by
LID Publishing
An imprint of LID Business Media Ltd.
LABS House, 15–19 Bloomsbury Way,
London, WC1A 2TH, UK

info@lidpublishing.com
www.lidpublishing.com

A member of:
BPR
businesspublishersroundtable.com

ISBN: 978-1-917391-59-7
ISBN: 978-1-917391-60-3 (ebook)

Cover and page design: Caroline Li

THE MIRROR NEVER LIES

FROM REFLECTION TO PROSPERITY – THE BLUEPRINT FOR SUCCESS AND FULFILMENT

IVAN BARTOLO

LID

MADRID | MEXICO CITY | LONDON
BUENOS AIRES | BOGOTA | SHANGHAI

The mirror does not lie with you in its path.

You see what you choose to see. Often, that is when the lie about your self-image is conceived.

Embrace the truth reflected in your own eyes, for in its clarity lies the power to transform the lies you have believed. See yourself not as you fear, but as you truly are, and begin the journey to your greatest self.

DEDICATION

My faith has been the greatest challenge of my life. No matter how earnestly I strive to walk the straight and narrow, my doubts, my questions, my imperfections, and even my thoughts have often stood as stumbling blocks between my Creator and myself.

Yet, when I reflect on my roots, my childhood, my youth, and objectively consider what my journey could have been in contrast to what it truly is, I know without a shadow of doubt that God has walked beside me every step of the way. The evidence lies in the blessings I received on the day I married my wife, Marthese, and in the extraordinary friendship I share with my three children: Kyle, Martina, and Anthony.

To Marthese, my pillar of strength, my unwavering source of love and support, this book is dedicated to you. Your faith in me has been a guiding light, and your love my greatest blessing. Thank you for walking this path with me.

With all my love and gratitude.

CONTENTS

1

FOREWORD

In business, there is a well-known truth forecasting is often the art of saying what will happen and then crafting good explanations for why it did not. The reality is that many companies set ambitious goals, only to fall short due to unforeseen challenges, shifting priorities, or internal inefficiencies.

So, when I first encountered 6PM PLC, a software development and services company based in Malta, predominantly selling to the UK NHS, I noticed something unusual. This was a company that made plans, set timeframes and then, months later, had not only met those deadlines but beaten them. That kind of disciplined execution is rare. As someone who has spent decades in the international software sector, particularly in mergers and acquisitions, I have met hundreds of executives and studied thousands of companies. The ability to deliver ahead of schedule was something I had rarely seen. I needed to know more. I needed to meet the person steering this ship.

That was how I first came across Ivan Bartolo.

Our first meeting was, in hindsight, both amusing and telling. I had already had multiple face-to-face meetings with one of 6PM's directors, yet when I was introduced to Ivan, I was mistakenly called 'Edward.' I did not correct it. Instead, I listened. Ivan was polite and brief, introducing himself and the company. When it was my turn, I presented a few slides with ideas and insights into the market.

Ivan did not interrupt. He listened carefully and then asked four or five precise questions, allowing me time to answer each one. Then he simply said, "*I think we need to meet. I'd like you to come to Malta next week.*"

The following morning, I received an email from his PA. Attached was a two-day schedule, broken down into meticulous 60- and 90-minute slots, complete with travel details and hotel arrangements. It was clear that I was dealing with someone who valued precision, structure and efficiency. The reason 6PM consistently delivered on its promises was becoming evident. It was embedded in its leadership.

A week later, I was in Malta. That first evening, Ivan and his CFO, Adrian, met me for dinner. It was not a business meeting, it was a conversation, a deep exchange of ideas, experiences and stories. By the end of the evening, well past 11.30 pm, I felt as if I had known Ivan for years. Before we parted ways, he looked at me and said, "I think we will be doing business together."

That statement became a reality.

From 2015 to 2017, we worked closely together, navigating the ups and downs of deal-making, overcoming frustrations and silencing doubters. Finally, after years of perseverance, 6PM PLC was acquired by Idox PLC in one of the largest transactions of its kind in Malta. There were many moments when people said the deal would never happen, but Ivan had something that many lack: determination, resilience, and an unshakable belief in his vision.

Over the years, I have had the privilege of working with many great clients, some of whom have become lifelong friends. Ivan is one of the very best. He is a man who is never afraid to stand up and speak (and, trust me, he can talk), but he also knows the rare art of when to listen. He started as my client, but a decade later, I am proud to call him my friend.

When Ivan asked me for feedback on *The Mirror Never Lies*, I gave it to him straight. Most people, when they ask for feedback, really mean, "Say something nice and make me feel good." That is not me. I told him what I truly thought. The book was excellent, but it could be even better with more of him in it. I knew he would take my critique with the same grace, old-world politeness, and charm that I have come to admire. He thanked me, considered my comments, and made some changes. I have been in business for many decades, having completed M&A deals across four continents, experiencing both failure and success. When my daughter Rebecca recently came to me for advice as she embarked on her own entrepreneurial journey, my final piece of guidance was simple. Read *The Mirror Never Lies.*

I can think of no higher recommendation for this book.

My only real criticism? That he does not mention me, because I taught Ivan everything he knows. Joking aside, to Ivan, I say thank you. Here's to our next adventure.

Mark Edwards
CEO, Boss Equity
Strategic Positioning Consultant & M&A Specialist
Author of *Competitive Space Positioning*

2

FOUNDATION

LOOK IN THE MIRROR. DISCOVER YOUR BEST SELF

In today's relentless, fast-paced world, it is easy to lose sight of who you are and who you are capable of becoming. Routines take over, reflection gets sidelined, and potential remains untapped. ***The Mirror Never Lies*** is your wake-up call. It is a powerful invitation to encourage you to pause, look inward, and take charge of your journey. This is not just a book; it is your blueprint for transformation, designed to help you move from where you are to where you truly want to be.

While ***The Mirror Never Lie***s is a book that meets anyone, anywhere, it was written with a deep focus on the unique challenges faced by Gen Z and Millennials. Not because other generations are less important, nor because younger generations are inferior; quite the opposite. The author recognizes that Gen Z and Millennials are navigating an era of unprecedented change, shaped by technological advancements, the rise of social media, and global events like the Twin Towers attack and COVID-19.

Social media has redefined identity, success, and connection, creating both opportunities and pressures that previous generations never encountered. The curated nature of online life fuels comparison, self-doubt, and the constant chase for external validation. At the same time, the rapid rise of artificial intelligence, intelligent automation, and robotics is reshaping career paths, making adaptability and continuous learning more critical than ever.

Alongside these shifts, mental health is no longer a hidden struggle. It is a reality that must be acknowledged and addressed. Anxiety, burnout, and the pressures of modern living have given rise to a new level of awareness about emotional wellbeing. This book provides the structure, tools, and mindset to help young professionals and future leaders not just adapt but thrive, mentally, emotionally, and professionally in a world that continues to evolve at an unprecedented pace.

Read this book with the belief and hope that your best is always ahead of you, that the best version of yourself awaits you.

Pause for a moment and ask yourself a simple, yet challenging question:

> ***"Am I truly living my life to its fullest, or am I nestled in the comfort of what I already know?"***

Have you ever stopped and asked yourself this question?

For many, life becomes a quiet descent into routine, where curiosity fades and personal growth slows. You might think this statement is extreme, but honestly ask yourself:

> ***"Do I dedicate even a few minutes each day to self-reflection with the intention of personal growth?"***

"How often do I gaze into the mirror not just to see my reflection, but to recognize, challenge, and improve myself?"

Many individuals unknowingly stop learning at age 30, settling into familiar patterns that no longer challenge them. But growth is always possible if you choose to pursue it.

There are three types of people:

1. Those who never stop learning, constantly growing, and evolving.

2. Those who believe learning ends with formal education, stuck in their past knowledge.

3. Those who want to grow but feel overwhelmed, unsure where to begin or how to stay on track.

This book is for the third group, those who seek progress but need a clear, structured approach to achieve it.

Progress begins with clarity and focus. What gets measured improves. Personal Success Metrics (PSMs) act as your Google Maps for life, signposts that guide you with precision to fulfil your purpose and goals.

This book will show you how to create and track PSMs tailored to your unique purpose, goals, and aspirations, ensuring that every step you take is intentional and moves you closer to your desirable success.

The greatest barrier to self-improvement is not a lack of desire, it is a lack of clarity, measurement, and consistency. That is where this book comes in.

Unlike books that rely solely on motivation, ***The Mirror Never Lies*** provides a structured road map for personal transformation. Through daily practice, this book will help you to acquire a positive habit that will lead you to transform yourself.

Track your progress using PSMs, your clear, measurable steps toward your goals. Embrace the Thriveon habit, a simple but powerful process to review wins, extract lessons, and make changes daily.

Break free from stagnation by actively measuring, refining, and adapting to your growth.

This book does not just encourage you to reflect; it gives you the tools to take action. The Thriveon Digital Ecosystem (www.thriveon.vip) provides you with the tools you need to embark on a journey that will lead you to meeting the best version of yourself.

Where Does Your Penny Drop? Once again, ask yourself:

> ***"Do I dedicate even a few minutes each day to self-reflection with the intention of personal growth?"***

> ***"Am I taking intentional steps toward a better version of myself?"***

In the absence of this commitment, self-awareness and self-accountability begin to fade. Before you know it, you may find yourself stuck where the fear of change becomes your greatest thief, and the comfort zone becomes the biggest lie in your life's journey.

But here is the truth: your best self is not behind you, it is ahead of you.

This book is a guide to help you break free from complacency, ignite passion for self-growth, and embrace the continuous journey of becoming your best self.

It is time to look in the mirror with clear eyes, an open mind, and a willing heart. Your true potential awaits discovery.

So, here is your invitation to take a hard look to step beyond your comfort zone and seek the better version of yourself that is waiting just beyond your doubts. Welcome to your journey of discovery and transformation.

With encouragement and hope.

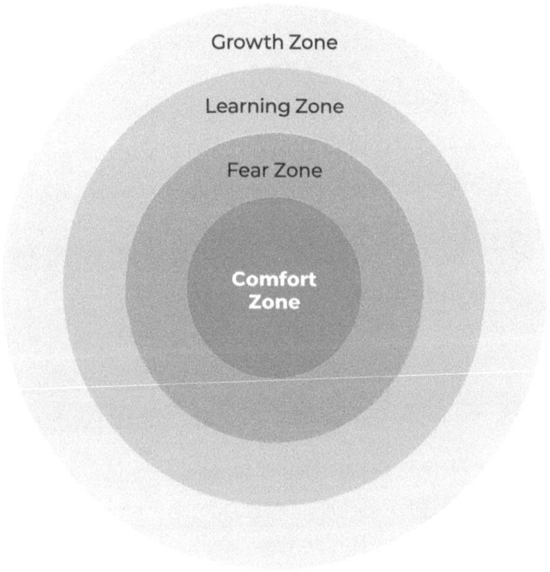

The comfort zone is like weeds in a garden. It grows quickly, overtaking everything in its path that is meant for meaningful growth.

3

INTRODUCTION

Welcome to a journey of self-discovery and transformation. In today's fast-paced world, where distractions and responsibilities pull us in every direction, it is easy to slip into autopilot, living but not truly growing. This book is your invitation to take a good look at yourself and take control of your personal growth.

Personal growth is not a single event but a daily practice. It is a process of continuous refinement. This book reflects this truth, encouraging you to slow down, assess, adjust, and align your actions with your purpose and goals each day.

Throughout these chapters, you will encounter intentional repetition of key principles. This is by design, a reminder that growth is cyclical, not linear, and that lasting change comes from consistent effort and self-reflection.

Just as a sailor makes continuous course corrections to stay on course, you must recalibrate your thoughts, choices, and behaviours to remain aligned with your aspirations. Embrace this rhythm of reflection and it will deepen your understanding and bring you closer to your best self, one step at a time.

The Mirror Never Lies challenges you to dive deep into the mirror of self-reflection, not just to see who you are, but to discover who you can become. It is about moving from good to great through intentional reflection, structured goal setting, and a commitment to continuous personal development.

At the core of this book lies the Thriveon Method, a simple yet powerful daily self-reflection positive habit designed to turn awareness into action. In just 20–30 minutes a day, you will answer four essential questions that will help you celebrate wins, learn from setbacks, refine your approach, and stay on track toward your goals. This is not just about self-awareness; it is about building momentum for lasting growth.

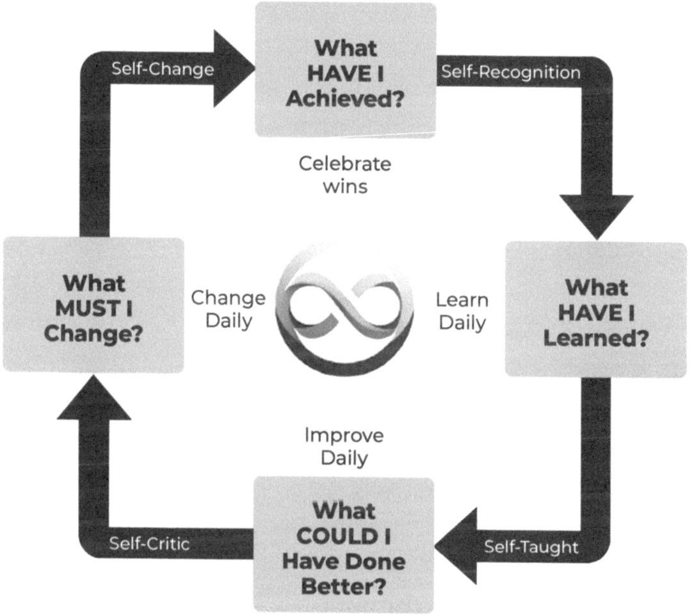

What is not measured does not improve. This fundamental truth applies universally, whether in business, health, or personal growth. While routines provide stability, they can also lead to stagnation, keeping you stuck in a comfort zone that limits progress. The Thriveon Method breaks this cycle by introducing structure to the unstructured through finding purpose, goal setting, and a clear process for measuring growth.

Think of your goals as the destination on a journey and your PSMs as the signposts that guide you along the way. These metrics provide clarity and motivation, helping you track progress and make necessary adjustments. For example, if your goal is career growth, a PSM might be attending three networking events this quarter or earning a certification by year's end. By breaking big aspirations into smaller, actionable steps, you stay focused and build confidence with each milestone achieved.

And the best part? Every step forward is a celebration of progress bringing you closer to the life you envision.

Your best self is not behind you, it is ahead of you. The question is: are you actively working toward it, or are you waiting for change to happen?

If you are already on this journey, keep going. If not, it is time to start now.

Before delving deeper into my passion for people's growth and fulfilment, I want to share a story with you, a powerful, real-life example that perfectly embodies the principles in this book. It is a testament to why the journey to becoming the best version of yourself is always worth pursuing.

While writing this book throughout 2024, I found myself enjoying the Christmas and New Year's festive season, unwinding with YouTube on my TV. That is when I stumbled upon an artist I had never heard of before, a testament, perhaps, to my age. Her name? Dua Lipa. The video was titled "An Evening with Dua Lipa (Live from the Royal Albert Hall.)"[1] The title itself caught my attention. Performing at the Royal Albert Hall is no small feat; it is a stage for the extraordinary. I clicked, curious to see what this young artist had to offer.

What followed left me utterly captivated. Dua Lipa, with her mesmerizing voice, undeniable confidence, and striking presence, completely stole the show. But what struck me even more was the sheer joy radiating from everyone in that iconic venue. The audience was alive, the musicians were thriving, and Dua herself was a beacon of energy. It was a celebration of humanity, a burst of positive energy we all deserve to experience. I could not look away.

While every moment of that performance was remarkable, two segments left a profound impact on me.

The Power of Radical Optimism (minute 20:10 to 23:46). In this part of the concert commentary, Dua shared her thoughts on her new album, *Radical Optimism*, calling it one of the best experiences of her life. Her sincerity was palpable, not just in her words but in her body language, and tone. “We are all so proud,” she said, emphasizing team success even though she was the star. She exuded humility and leadership, celebrating her journey and those who supported her.

She spoke about her school days, reminiscing, “Music was just a dream in the playground at school.” It is clear she never stopped chasing her best self. Then came a touching moment: the introduction of Ray, her music schoolteacher and mentor. Ray’s wisdom resonated deeply with me, echoing the philosophy of *The Mirror Never Lies*. He said, “If you are only doing the things that are comfortable to you, I just do not think the boundaries stretch enough.” Growth, he reminded us, happens outside the comfort zone. He admitted to deliberately challenging Dua with difficult tasks to help her strive for greatness.

After nearly a decade apart, Dua and Ray reunited. It was a poignant moment filled with gratitude and mutual admiration. Dua reflected on how his guidance shaped her, saying, "I think it is the reason why I am here now." Looking at Ray, she added, "You put me out of my comfort zone. Even to this day, where I excel is out of my comfort zone, it is where I grow." Her words are a testament to the transformative power of stepping beyond what is comfortable, a lesson that underscores the importance of daily self-reflection and the belief that our best is always ahead of us.

A Walk Down Memory Lane in New York (minute 34:25 to 37:30). In another unforgettable segment, Dua shared a nostalgic moment in New York City. After enjoying pizza with friends, she revisited a small venue where she had performed for the first time in the city back in 2016. The visit was deeply emotional. Standing before a microphone set at her height from years ago, she physically saw how much she has grown, not just in stature but as an artist.

She described how, in those early days, she performed "with no inhibitions," fully connecting with her music and purpose. This raw, fearless connection was key to her evolution. She also reflected on how those humble venues had grown with her, reinforcing the importance of perseverance and giving time its due. Her journey was a powerful reminder that growth takes time but, with persistence, the results are extraordinary.

Following this moment of reflection, I was reminded of Dua's immediate response after winning the Grammy Award for Best New Artist. On that global stage, she shared these profound words: "A big thank you to my fans who have allowed me to become the best version of myself." Think about that for a moment. She had just achieved one of the highest accolades in the music industry, and her first words were about striving to be her best self. How awesome is that? Of course, she humbly thanked her fans, which is noble, but the unspoken message was equally powerful: she believed in herself and embraced the journey to come face-to-face with her purpose in life.

An Evening to Remember. As the concert drew to a close, I sat in my living room, filled with admiration for this incredible young artist. Dua Lipa's music was fantastic, her voice stunning, but what stood out most was her vibrant energy. The magic she created that night in the Royal Albert Hall transcended the screen and filled my home with its warmth and vitality.

> **Brava, Dua**. You have reminded me, and so many others, that true growth lies in embracing challenges, pursuing purpose, and believing that our best is yet to come.

For over 25 years, I have had the privilege of traveling across the United States, Canada, Europe, the United Kingdom, and Scandinavia, working with diverse organizations to deliver management training in business agility. Along the way, I engaged with thousands of individuals, each interaction enriching my own understanding of human potential. A striking pattern emerged; most adults settle comfortably within their perceived limits, unknowingly confined by their own comfort zones. The real tragedy? Many are completely unaware that they have stopped striving for their best selves.

In every class I taught, I was fortunate to be enriched by the diverse experiences of each participant, a reminder that everyone has something valuable to teach. I gained countless insights from the thousands of remarkable individuals I had the privilege to meet. Yet, despite their talents and potential, I often observed a common struggle: many people, regardless of background, culture, or stage in life, gave only superficial attention to their own self-development and fulfilment.

Why do I say this? Each time, I passionately introduced the Thriveon process to encourage people to embrace and acquire this positive habit of mine. I quickly realized something unsettling. Many had never truly considered their own self-development or personal growth. It was as if life had pulled them into a vacuum of artificial comfort, a state where people settled for what life served them, knowing there was more, but believing it was meant for others.

The Thriveon habit outlined in this book is a structured self-reflection daily process. A simple yet profound routine, it consists of four daily questions designed to be completed in just 20 to 30 minutes. Without exception, participants recognized its value and responded with enthusiasm. Yet, when I asked the next day who had attempted the exercise, the responses painted a different picture. Some avoided the question, as if they had not heard it. Others admitted they had tried but found it difficult. And some had started but stopped, uncertain of how to answer the four questions.

Those who ignored the process often believed they were already the best version of themselves, a limiting mindset that kept them anchored in their comfort zone, unknowingly depriving themselves of their full potential. Those who tried but struggled showed a willingness to grow but encountered familiar obstacles. I empathized with them. I, too, struggled when I first began, facing moments of self-doubt.

It is easy to dismiss self-reflection, to avoid the discomfort of truly examining yourself. But, often, the real challenge is not the process itself; it is the lack of knowledge of one's own purpose in life, the absence of clear goals, and the failure to define meaningful Personal Success Metrics (PSMs). Without these guiding elements, self-reflection can feel aimless or even frustrating. So, when participants expressed difficulty, I encouraged them to first define their purpose, write down their personal and professional goals, establish meaningful PSMs, and then revisit the four questions.

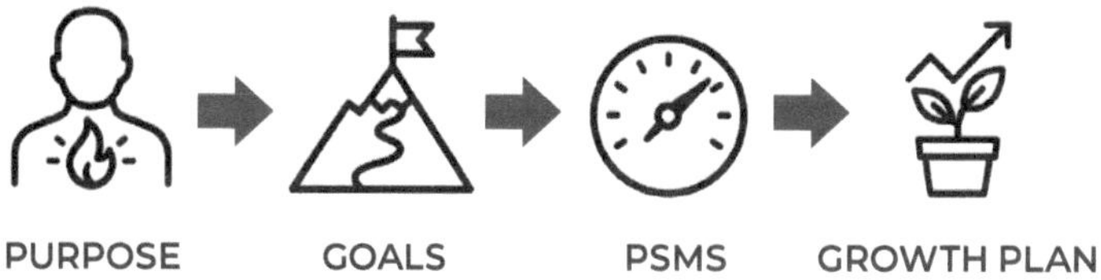

Invariably, a lightbulb moment would occur. Clarity replaced hesitation, and even the sceptics, those who had initially resisted, began embracing the Thriveon Method with renewed appreciation and commitment.

At the end of each training course, I always asked myself: after our time together, how many participants will truly commit to embedding this self-reflection practice into their daily lives with the discipline and consistency it demands?

That is the real test of growth.

Everyone navigates life with its challenges, balancing both work-related and personal concerns each day. Our minds are constantly occupied with tasks, deadlines, workplace dynamics, financial responsibilities, and personal well being. For many, work or study-related thoughts dominate up to 70% of their waking hours during the workweek, though some actively compartmentalize them to maintain a sense of balance in life. Personal reflections such as family responsibilities, health, and long-term goals tend to surface more in the mornings, evenings, and weekends, filling the remaining mental space.

Are you one of these individuals? Before you answer, look in the mirror; remember, it never lies.

For many, this constant stream of thoughts remains unstructured and undocumented. If challenged, they would likely realize that the lack of structure and visibility makes it difficult to track personal and professional progress. Without a clear way to measure growth, motivation fades, and the comfort zone becomes an easy refuge.

And what happens in that comfort zone? It becomes a place where dissatisfaction festers, where it is easier to blame circumstances and others than to take ownership of change. Left unchecked, it leads to intellectual stagnation at age 30 and a slow, passive existence until physical burial at age 80.

Why Self-Reflection Matters. Reflecting on where you are in life is not always easy. It takes courage to confront your shortcomings and a genuine willingness to change. But growth begins with awareness. The moment you recognize your habits, thoughts, and actions, you reclaim the power to shape them. I trust that this book will help you understand that self-reflection, when done with intention, is not just a passive exercise. It is a powerful catalyst for transformation.

How Thriveon Supports Your Growth. Thriveon as in Thrive On. Imagine starting each day with clarity, purpose, and the confidence that you are moving closer to the life you want. That is the power of Thriveon. It is more than just a process; it is a way to infuse growth into every single day. Whether you are celebrating yesterday's wins, overcoming today's challenges, or envisioning tomorrow's possibilities, Thriveon provides the structure to turn small daily actions into meaningful progress. It is not just a method; it is your personal guide to living with purpose and courage.

A Commitment to Yourself. This is my invitation to you: make a commitment to yourself. Cultivate the discipline to look in the mirror each day, not just to see your reflection, but to truly see yourself, reflect, and grow. Challenge your beliefs about who you are, redefine your potential, and push beyond your comfort zone. The mirror does not lie, but it does reflect the person you are becoming shaped by the choices you make every day.

Embark on this journey from good to great. Witness your own transformation.

Start **today**. Start **now**.

SOMETHING TO PONDER

Living the same week
a few thousand times
and calling it **LIFE**?

Call to Action: This is a good time to reflect and take note of your thoughts.

1. **Chase Your Best Self**: Write one step you will take today to move closer to your future self.

2. **Pause and Reflect**: Take two minutes and ask, *"What did I learn about myself from reading this chapter?"*

3. **Invest in You**: Commit to one positive habit that will help you grow (e.g. reduce screen time). Start small, but start now.

4

THE THRIVEON METHOD

The Power of Reflection. Thriveon's approach to growth is rooted in self-reflection, and the core of the method is based on four essential questions that you must ask yourself each day. These questions are designed to foster self-awareness, accountability, and a forward-looking mindset, encouraging you to embrace every day as an opportunity for growth.

While this chapter focuses on the Thriveon process built around the four core questions, it is essential to approach this process with clarity. Clarity is knowing why you are pursuing growth, what you aim to achieve, and how you will measure progress. Without a clear purpose, meaningful goals and structured Personal Success Metrics (PSMs), self-reflection risks becoming an unstructured exercise rather than a powerful tool for transformation. You will find deeper guidance on defining your purpose in Chapter 7.

To follow the Thriveon Method, your full commitment is essential. This commitment begins with cultivating a positive attitude. But what does a 'positive attitude' truly mean in this context? Think of the English alphabet, where each letter is assigned a percentage value – A equals 1%, B equals 2%, and so on until Z where it equals 26%. The word **'attitude'** when converted (1% + 20% + 20% + 9% + 20% + 21% + 4% + 5%) totals a perfect 100%. This calculation beautifully symbolizes that a positive attitude involves you giving your all, your 100%.

Do not fool yourself into believing that you are doing more than you should or giving more than you possibly can. Thinking and claiming to give "more than 100%" is simply an illusion. Using the same conversion method, any such claim equates to 103%; quite literally, bullshit (2% + 21% + 12% + 12% + 19% + 8% + 9% + 20%). Honesty with yourself about what constitutes full effort is the cornerstone of true progress and growth.

In the Thriveon Method, giving your 100% means consistency. It is not just about attempting reflection when convenient but doing so daily, while also setting reasonable boundaries to avoid burnout, perhaps skipping weekends or public holidays. The four questions may appear simple, but without purpose, clear goals, and PSMs, they become significantly harder to answer meaningfully. This is why purpose, goals, and PSMs setting is pivotal. These form the foundation for a focused, purpose-driven self-reflection process. Without them, your efforts risk becoming vague and ineffective.

THE FOUR THRIVEON METHOD QUESTIONS

The four Thriveon questions are encouraging you to recognize yourself for your achievements, to be self-taught by reflecting on the lessons you learned, to positively critique yourself by identifying what, in fact, you could have done better and, finally, to self-change by listing what action you must take to change.

Thriveon Questions	**Purpose**	**Example Prompt**
Today, what did I achieve?	Celebrate accomplishments	"What progress did I make today?"
Toaday, what did I learn?	Extract lessons from experiences	"What new insights did I gain?"
Today, what could I have done better?	Identify areas for improvement	"Where could I improve now?"
What must I change?	Plan proactive adjustments	"What actions will I take next?"

At first glance, the Thriveon questions may seem simple. After all, they only ask you to reflect on what you have achieved, learned, could improve, and need to change. But their true power lies in their connection to your goals and PSMs that are fully aligned with your purpose. Without a clear vision of where you are heading or a structured way to measure progress, answering these questions can feel like searching for direction in the dark.

Consider this: How can you assess what you have achieved if you do not know what you are striving for? How can you improve if you have not defined what success looks like? The Thriveon questions are not just prompts; they are your daily guide to ensuring your efforts align with your aspirations.

When paired with well-defined goals and PSMs, these questions transform into a compass for growth. They challenge you to stay intentional, celebrate progress, and refine your path. Remember, clarity in your goals turns reflection into action. So, before you begin answering these questions, take the time to define your goals and structure your PSMs. The clearer your vision, the more impactful your answers will be.

The greatest adventure you can embark on is to discover your true self.

1. **Today, what did I achieve?** Reflect on your accomplishments and milestones reached toward your PSMs. Celebrating achievements, big or small, reinforces positive habits and builds self-confidence. By recognizing your daily wins, you are acknowledging progress, which fuels further motivation. **Learn how to self-recognize.**

   From my experience, I have seen the transformative power of celebrating wins in both professional and personal settings. For business owners, business leaders, and managers, I recommend that you install a **brass bell** at the office. Every time there is a win, be it closing a deal, completing a challenging project, or surpassing a goal, sound the bell. Gather the team, recognize the winner(s), and celebrate the moment. This practice not only fuels motivation but also creates a positive craving for success, turning achievements into a shared source of energy and pride.

   Individuals, the same applies to you. When you achieve something, however small, do not just acknowledge it, celebrate it. Treat yourself to something that gives you great pleasure or satisfaction. It could be enjoying your favourite dessert, taking a relaxing walk, or indulging in a hobby. These celebrations solidify the connection between effort and reward, building a positive feedback loop that encourages continuous progress.

Remember, achievements are the building blocks of your journey. Recognizing and celebrating them ensures that the foundation of your success is strong and enduring.

2. **Today, what did I learn?** Growth often comes from knowledge gained through successes, setbacks, and everyday experiences. This question encourages you to turn your day into a lesson, to see challenges as opportunities, and to recognize how each experience adds to your growth journey. **Learn more about the power of self-taught.**

    From my experience, learning new things is one of the most powerful ways to bring light and vitality into life. I encourage everyone to document what they have learned each day. Over a period of 24 to 60 months, revisiting these lessons is like looking at old photos of yourself; it becomes a vivid reminder of how far you have come, how much you have grown, and how you have evolved as a person.

    Additionally, I have seen great value in fostering collective learning environments. At work or within teams, committees, or groups,

I encourage organizing what I like to call a **'donut session'**, a weekly or monthly gathering where everyone gets an opportunity to share what they have learned. These sessions become rewarding moments where individuals can:

- Be recognized for their insights and contributions
- Teach others and reinforce their own learning
- Demonstrate and nurture the most important value in any organization: sharing knowledge.

When you commit to learning and sharing, you not only accelerate your own growth but also inspire those around you to do the same. Each lesson becomes a thread in the fabric of your journey, weaving a tapestry of continuous improvement and connection.

3. **Today, what could I have done better?** Self-improvement requires honest introspection. This question prompts you to examine any mistakes or areas where you fell short, not as a form of negative criticism but as a means of learning. By identifying areas for improvement, you foster resilience and a desire to move forward and make better choices. **Learn how to positively self-critique.**

From my experience, this question has been a cornerstone of my personal and professional growth. During a period when I was traveling nearly every week to deliver business agility training, I encountered a vast array of people, cultures, and organizations. Delivering the same course to a start-up versus a corporate organization required very different approaches. Start-ups often struggled with limited resources but thrived on agility and minimal bureaucracy. By contrast, corporates had ample resources but faced significant hurdles in navigating bureaucracy.

Each day, after delivering training, I made it a priority to reflect on my performance. What could I have done better? Did I fail to empathize with a participant's unique challenges? Could I have explained a concept more clearly? If a mistake required it, I did not hesitate to return the next day and apologize. That moment of humility not only built trust but also improved my delivery, resulting in better participant ratings and greater confidence in myself.

The most important outcome of this daily positive self-criticism was that it kept me on my toes. It challenged me to be better and fuelled my motivation to strive for excellence.

Mistakes, when acknowledged and learned from, become stepping-stones to growth rather than setbacks.

This practice is not about dwelling on what went wrong. Instead, it is about seeing those moments as opportunities to refine, adjust, and move closer to your best self. When you commit to honest introspection, you set the stage for continuous improvement and greater resilience in the face of challenges.

4. **What MUST I change?** This question allows you to set intentions for the way forward. This becomes your change actions log, things you must act upon. It encourages proactive thinking, reminding you that growth requires consistent action and adaptation. It gives you the chance to pivot, adjust your goals, and make necessary changes to stay on track. **Learn how to self-change.**

   From my experience, this question is incredibly important because it feeds directly into what I call your Change Actions Log. To truly grow and evolve, it is vital to track the changes you commit to making in a structured and deliberate way. I recommend maintaining a Change Actions Log in a simple tabular format that helps you capture and monitor your progress over time.

Your Change Actions Log should include these key elements:

- Why you need the change (what is the driving reason or motivation?)
- What are you going to change (be specific about the action or habit to modify)
- How you are going to change (define the steps you will take to implement change)
- By when are you going to change (set a deadline to maintain focus and accountability).

Just as importantly, apply change control as you progress. Periodically review your log to evaluate whether adjustments are needed to your current PSMs. Growth is a dynamic process, and staying flexible ensures that your goals remain aligned with your evolving priorities.

Why Change?	What Will I Change?	How Will I Change	By When	PSM Adjustment Needed?
My morning routine lacks structure, causing delays.	Create a consistent morning schedule.	Set a fixed wake-up time, plan tasks the night before.	Next 2 Weeks	Add a PSM: Wake up by 6.30 am daily.
My project deadlines are frequently missed.	Improve task prioritzation and time management.	Use a task management app to plan weekly goals.	1 month	Add a PSM: Complete tasks 24 hours in advance.
I have been neglecting my health due to work demands.	Exercise regularly and improve eating habits.	Schedule gym session 3x weekly and prepare meals.	Next 3 months	Update PSM: Track workouts weekly.
My teams struggle with communication during meetings.	Facilitate more structured team discussions.	Introduce an agenda and action points for every meeting.	Next team meeting	Adjust PSM: Measure meeting efficiency scores.
I feel disconnected from personal relationships.	Spend more intentional time with family and friends.	Block weekly time in my calendar for catchups.	Next 1 month	Add a PSM: Schedule at least 1 quality time activity weekly.

A Positive Habit for Consistent Growth. Daily reflection using these four questions helps you create a positive habit for self-awareness and personal growth. Thriveon integrates these questions into a daily practice, helping you maintain momentum by staying mindful of your journey. Reflection is a powerful tool; it encourages deeper engagement with your actions and reminds you that each day offers a fresh start.

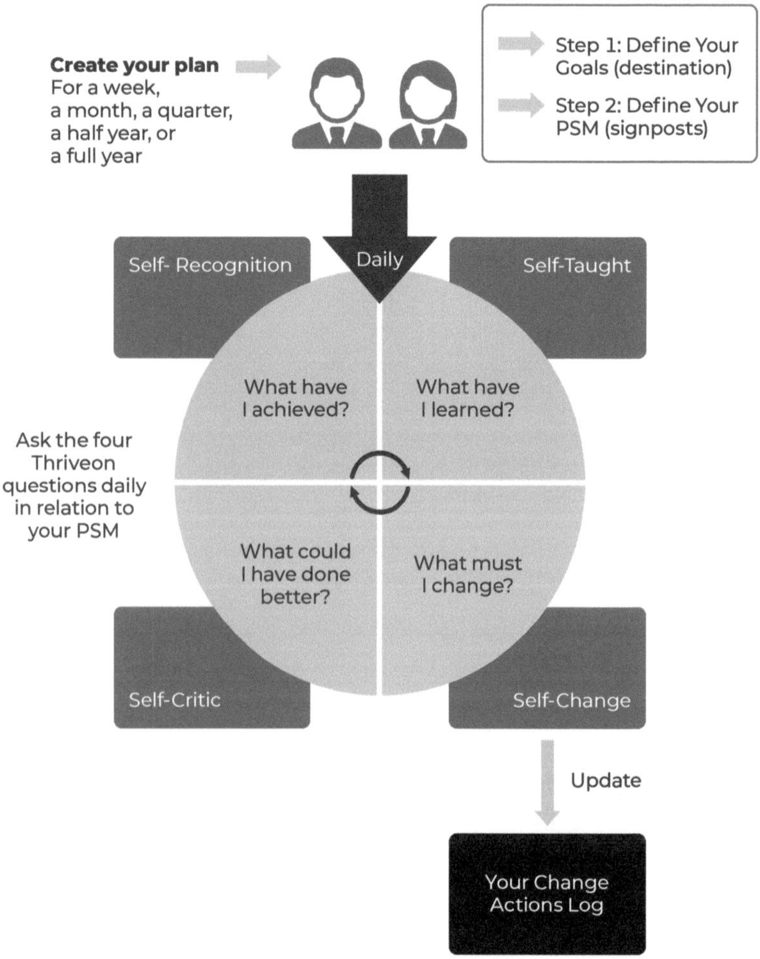
Create your plan
For a week,
a month, a quarter,
a half year, or
a full year
Step 1: Define Your Goals (destination)
Step 2: Define Your PSM (signposts)
Daily
Self- Recognition
Self-Taught
What have I achieved?
What have I learned?
Ask the four Thriveon questions daily in relation to your PSM
What could I have done better?
What must I change?
Self-Critic
Self-Change
Update
Your Change Actions Log

By integrating Thriveon's structured method into your daily routine, you can achieve a balance between introspection and action. A consistent reflection process ensures that your goals remain aligned with your evolving life purpose. This practice not only builds accountability, but also fosters a mindset of continuous improvement, empowering you to transition from routine to purposeful living and from good to great. Thriveon is designed to support you throughout your journey, offering clarity and actionable insights to help you celebrate progress and navigate challenges with confidence.

The Role of Failure in Reflection. As you practice the Thriveon Method, you will inevitably face moments when your self-reflection reveals that you achieved or learned nothing on any particular day. Such admissions may feel like failure, but they are, in fact, acts of honesty. Failure arises only when you abandon the process of reflection entirely, when you stop asking what you could have been done better (Question 3) and what must you change (Question 4).

Every entry under Question 3 should inspire at least one actionable item under Question 4. These actions become your change actions for personal growth, with each point accompanied by a specific timeline for implementation. Change without action is merely wishful thinking. True failure occurs not when you fall short of perfection, but when you neglect to take the steps necessary to evolve into the person you aspire to be.

From personal experience, committing to oneself and practicing daily self-reflection, a positive habit I have nurtured over the last 30 years, has been far from easy. There were moments when life pushed me into tight corners, when I lost my sense of purpose, when I doubted my ability to push myself into the next growth zone. In those moments, the allure of the comfort zone was strong, and I wanted to abandon this habit altogether and simply stop caring.

Yet, in those dark moments, the only fuel left in my tank was the small light ignited by faith, a steadfast belief that my best is always ahead of me. That flicker of hope reminded me that while there are countless reasons to give up, there are always more reasons to keep marching forward.

As the years piled up and the grey streaks in my hair became more prominent, I began to understand that my commitment to self-reflection was my guiding star. It remained constant, shining through the haze of doubt and the storms of life. Of course, there were patches, days, weeks and months when I felt I had achieved nothing, learned nothing, and arrogantly believed there was nothing I could have done better. But even in those moments, it was perseverance and discipline that kept me anchored.

> I have come to learn that life's path is not a straight line. My journey has been a zigzag of ups and downs, requiring constant adjustments to my sails. But through it all, I have discovered the beauty of witnessing my own growth. This process has taught me that progress is not about perfection, it is about persistence, resilience, and the courage to keep evolving. With each reflection, I have inched closer to becoming a better version of myself, and that alone has made the commitment worthwhile.

Reflection is a journey, not a destination. By committing to this daily practice and holding yourself accountable to change, you will witness profound growth. Remember, the mirror never lies. It reflects not only who you are but who you have the potential to become. Let the Thriveon Method be your guide to unlocking that potential.

SOMETHING TO PONDER

Discipline bears the important fruit of self-respect that provides you with the ability to say no to oneself.

Call to Action: This is a good time to reflect and take note of your thoughts.

1. **Start Small**: Dedicate ten minutes each evening to reflect on your day. Write down one win, one lesson, and one step that leads to change.

2. **Stay Consistent**: Commit to practicing this reflection daily for the next seven days. Track your progress and notice how you feel at the end of the week.

3. **Grow with Purpose**: Set one specific, measurable goal for this month, and use your daily reflections to stay accountable and adapt as needed.

TAKE THE NEXT STEP IN YOUR JOURNEY

To fully experience the power of the **Thriveon Method**, it is recommended that you engage with the chapter's exercise, available for free on the **Thriveon Digital Ecosystem**.

This exercise is more than just an activity, it is a transformational tool designed to help you bridge the gap between knowledge and action. The insights you gain will enhance your understanding of this chapter, reinforce your goals, and set you up for lasting growth.

Before moving on to the next chapter, give yourself this moment of reflection.

The best version of you is waiting; take the first step today.

5

THE POWER OF PSMS

Measuring growth, defining progress, and taking control of your journey is easily achievable. Growth that is not measured is easily forgotten. Without a way to track progress, even the best intentions can fade into wishful thinking. This is why Personal Success Metrics (PSMs) are essential for intentional personal growth.

PSMs brings structure, clarity, and accountability to your self-improvement journey. Originally developed to measure business productivity and organizational success, performance metrics has evolved into a powerful tool for personal development. Just as businesses track their efficiency, individuals can measure progress in areas like health, relationships, mindset, and career growth.

By defining what success looks like, PSMs ensure that personal growth is not just an idea but a measurable, achievable reality.

The origins and evolution of performance metrics known as Key Performance Indicators (KPIs) are now a cornerstone of personal and professional development, but their origins stretch back centuries, evolving to meet the needs of growing complexity in organizational and individual achievement. Understanding their history provides valuable context for why they were created and why they remain relevant today, especially in the context of personal growth, as emphasized in this book.

The Evolution of Measuring Progress. While Personal Success Metrics (PSMs) are a relatively new concept in personal development, their foundations trace back centuries, evolving to meet the changing needs of individuals and organizations alike.

Ancient Foundations – Measuring Progress Before It Had a Name. The idea of tracking progress is not new. Ancient civilizations such as the Egyptians and Babylonians used structured systems to evaluate agricultural yields, taxation, and construction projects. These early forms of measurement helped leaders assess success, course-correct, and make informed decisions. The same principles used today in personal growth tracking.

The Industrial Revolution – Productivity and Efficiency Take Centre Stage. During the Industrial Revolution, structured measurement became essential. Factories needed clear ways to track output, efficiency, and profitability. In the 19th century, Frederick Winslow Taylor introduced scientific management, emphasizing task optimization and time efficiency, one of the first formal uses of performance metrics in organizations.[2] At this stage, KPIs (Key Performance Indicators) were created to align tasks with broader goals, ensuring that businesses functioned effectively and efficiently.

The 20th Century – From Business Efficiency to Strategic Growth. By the mid-20th century, KPIs were no longer just about productivity: they became tools for strategy and growth.

- Peter Drucker, often called the father of modern management, introduced Management by Objectives (MBO) in the 1950s, emphasizing that clear goals, coupled with measurement, drive success.[3]
- The Balanced Scorecard, developed by Robert Kaplan and David Norton in the 1990s, expanded KPIs beyond financial metrics to customer satisfaction, internal processes, and learning and growth.[4]

This shift was profound. It showed that metrics were not just about output but about long-term success. This same shift is now happening in personal development.

The Shift from Business KPIs to Personal Success Metrics (PSMs). While KPIs were originally designed for businesses, their true power lies in personal application. Organizations still use KPIs or OKRs (Objectives and Key Results) to measure growth, efficiency, and impact. But what about your own life? If businesses need structured tracking to succeed, shouldn't individuals apply the same logic to their goals, habits, and aspirations? This is where Personal Success Metrics (PSMs) come in. PSMs are the personal evolution of KPIs, a structured way to ensure that your growth is measured, trackable, and intentional.

Why Do Personal Success Metrics (PSMs) Matter? PSMs were created for the same reason KPIs were; that is, to make progress visible, measurable, and actionable. Whether you are improving your fitness, relationships, career, or mindset, tracking your progress using PSMs ensures that you are always moving forward.

PSMs help you to:

- **Gain Clarity** – Clearly define what success means to you
- **Create Accountability** – Stay committed to your personal growth
- **Drive Continuous Improvement** – Reflect, adapt, and evolve
- **Align Your Actions with Your Purpose** – Ensure your effort is meaningful.

PSMs in the Context of the Thriveon Method. The Thriveon Method integrates Purpose, Goals, and PSMs into a personal growth plan. PSMs are used not as a rigid corporate tool, but as a signpost toward personal success.

- Your Purpose (why) gives your life meaning
- Your Goals (what) define the path ahead
- Your PSMs (how) ensure progress toward your purpose.

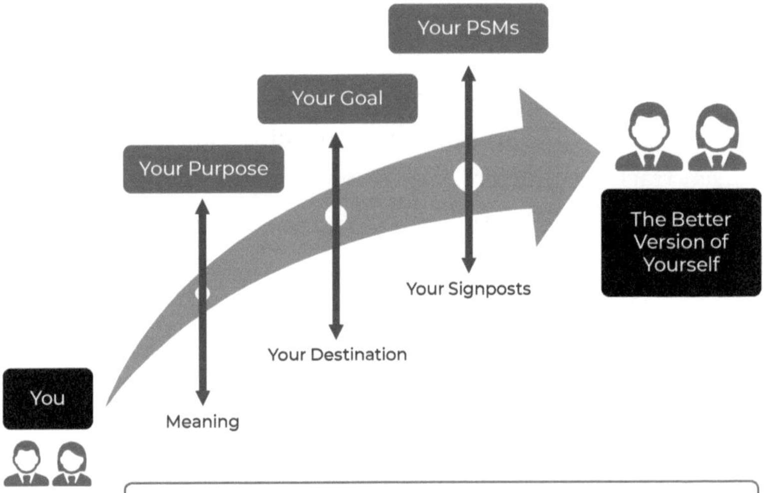

Construction Formulas

Purpose Statement:
I [**Verb**] to [**Contribution**] by using my passion [**Passions**] while honouring my core [**Values**].

Goal Statement:
[**Verb**] + [**Achievement**] + [**Specific Outcome**] + [**By When**]

PSMs Statement:
[**Verb**] + [**Action**] + [**Target**] + [**By When**]

From tracking fitness milestones, career achievements, or personal habits, PSMs bridge the gap between intention and action.

PSMs are not about perfection, they are about progress. By embracing measurable self-improvement, you take control of your own growth, ensuring that every step brings you closer to the best version of yourself.

I am fully convinced of one truth. What is measured improves. Goals and PSMs are your critical success factors to enable you to achieve success, diagnose your challenges accurately, make effective decisions, and foster a constructive approach that continually leads you to discover your best self.

At first glance, you might interpret this statement to mean that something will improve simply because you measure it daily. However, it does not work that way. Improvement requires a structured approach. Each goal (destination) must be broken down into measurable PSMs (signposts), which act as the building blocks for success.

A goal without clarity is like a ship without a rudder, adrift and uncertain of its destination. To create meaningful and actionable goals, they must be supported by SMART (Specific, Measurable, Achievable, Relevant, and Time-bound) PSMs. At the heart of the PSMs definition statement lies the critical role of verbs, which transform vague aspirations into clear, actionable commitments.

To create clear and actionable PSMs, follow this simple formula:

PSMs Statement =
[Verb] + [Action] + [Target] + [By When]

This formula ensures that your PSMs are specific, measurable, and aligned with your goals. The table below provides a better understanding to the formula elements.

Component	Detail	Explanation
Verb	Use an action verb like Achieve, Increase, Reduce, **Complete**, Lose, or Maintain.	The verb defines the intention of the PSMs. It clearly specifies what you aim to do.
Action	Add the PSMs Description to the Action. ***Example: gym workouts.***	This is where you describe the specific action you want to take.
Target	Add the PSMs Target ***Example: quantity five.***	The target specifies the measurable result you aim to achieve for a specific frequency.
By When	Add the PSMs Target Frequency. ***Example: per week.***	This sets the timeline or frequency for completing the PSMs.

The example PSM in the table would finally read, "Complete five gym workouts per week" for a goal related to physical fitness.

Consider a common goal such as 'reduce weight.' The goal expresses the intent of wanting to reduce one's weight, but it is very loose, and it lacks precision and focus. The role of the PSM is to make it SMART: "Reduce five kilos within 12 weeks from now" or, "Reduce five kilos by the end of March 20XX." These statements include the four key elements explained again below:

1. **Verb**: A verb like "reduce" signals the precise action to be taken.

2. **Action**: Add the action description to the verb, "reduce weight."

3. **Target**: The specific outcome or achievement; in this case, five kilos.

4. **Time Frame**: A defined period, providing urgency and a clear endpoint.

By anchoring PSMs with these components, you turn intentions into actionable plans, making progress measurable and accountability tangible. Remember, every goal is a promise to yourself, a commitment to act with purpose. So, use strong verbs, define your targets, and set timelines that inspire action. This simple yet powerful formula ensures your aspirations are not just dreams but destinations you are actively working toward.

For example, let's take a more well-defined and structured goal and witness how PSMs support this goal with more precise actionable focus.

The goal is to "Lose five kilos within 12 weeks from now." The following are the specific PSMs that support this goal:

- PSM 1 - Walk and burn a minimum of 600 calories per day.
- PSM 2 - Complete three one-hour weight training sessions at the gym per week.
- PSM 3 -Avoid consuming any calories from carbohydrates daily.
- PSM 4 - Do not exceed 2,000 calories per day, spread across breakfast, lunch, and a light dinner.
- PSM 5 - Measure weight bi-weekly (every other Monday at 7 am).

The single goal has been broken into five actionable, measurable steps. Each PSM is SMART. To avoid failure and disappointment, it is essential to ensure that your PSMs are realistic. For example, if PSM 4 had been set at 200 calories per day, while still measurable and time-bound, it would be unrealistic and harmful to your health.

Tracking these PSMs provides valuable insights. By measuring PSM 1, 3, and 4 daily, PSM 2 weekly, and PSM 5 bi-weekly, you gather data to understand your progress. You might notice improvements in how quickly you burn 600 calories or develop better control over your calorie intake.

When you acquire bi-weekly weight measurement through PSM 5, you can assess whether you are on track to achieve your goal within 12 weeks. If you are not on track, you can adjust: like increasing your calorie burn, reducing your daily calorie intake to 1,800, or introducing a new PSM related to intermittent fasting.

This example illustrates the power of PSMs in achieving personal goals. Whether your goal is weight loss, professional growth, or personal development, the Thriveon Method encourages you to identify your goals, decompose them into measurable actions, and reflect daily on your progress.

A Personal Example: Growing Confidence Through PSMs. When I moved to London for work, I set personal development goals that changed my life. I had always struggled with making small talk. I was either too shy, too lazy, or lacked confidence. I did not like that version of myself and aspired to improve. To tackle this, I set two PSMs:

1. Speak to someone new every day, whether at the office, the supermarket, or on the London Underground.

2. Visit a local pub in Hatton Cross once a week and socialize with people working in the same business park.

> These PSMs, mapped to my goals to increase 'confidence' and 'grow my personal network,' forced me out of my comfort zone. They were not just about conversations; they were about building confidence and expanding my network. Over time, these small but deliberate actions had a profound impact. I became more self-assured, made valuable connections, and opened doors to new opportunities.

The Dynamic Nature of Goals and PSMs. Goals and PSMs are not static. They evolve as your priorities and aspirations change. While your goals and PSMs will change from time to time, the Thriveon Method remains your constant, a structured commitment to self-reflection and growth.

For all these years, I maintained the positive habit of documenting my Thriveon reflections in a diary. I would divide each page into four quadrants for the Thriveon questions, ensuring I stayed disciplined in tracking my progress. Looking back over three decades of self-reflection, I see not only how my goals evolved but also how this discipline and structure transformed me.

The journey has taken me from good to great, helping me achieve fulfilment and even self-actualization. By committing to measurable goals and self-reflection, you can chart a similar path, one of continuous improvement, meaningful progress, and personal growth.

While traditional work-related KPIs are designed to align with an organization's objectives, PSMs are entirely tailored to your own growth and fulfillment. They typically focus on areas in your life such as:

- **Personal Development** (growth in mindset, skills, and self-awareness)
- **Wellbeing** (mental, emotional, and overall life balance)
- **Career and Professional Growth** (advancement of career goals, leadership, and impact)
- **Physical Health Fitness** (strength, endurance, and active living)
- **Nutrition Dietary Habits** (healthy eating and sustainable nutrition practices)
- **Relationship and Social Growth** (building and nurturing meaningful connections)
- **Financial Growth Wealth Management** (growing assets, managing finances wisely)
- **Learning and Knowledge Expansion** (continual education, curiosity, and intellectual growth)
- **Contribution Impact** (making a positive difference through actions and service)
- **Spiritual Purpose-Driven Growth** (living with intention, values, and deeper connection)

When defining your PSMs, it is best to articulate them using clear and actionable language to ensure they are specific, measurable, and focused. The following are some examples of PSMs for different focus areas.

1. **Wellbeing PSM**: Meditation practice, sleep quality, social interactions, and daily hydration. For instance, set a target to meditate for ten minutes daily and track completion as Yes or No.

2. **Physical Fitness PSM**: Step goals, strength training, cardio, and stretching routines. An example could be aiming for 10,000 steps daily, tracked with a fitness app.

3. **Dietary PSM**: Vegetable intake, sugar reduction and water consumption. Set a goal like eating five servings of vegetables per day and log your progress.

4. **Personal Development PSM**: Reading, skill development, journaling, and learning new languages. For instance, set a target to read for 30 minutes a day and track your reading time.

In the introduction of this book, I shared my experience about the individuals who attended my Business Agility training sessions, where I introduced the Thriveon Method and the four self-reflection questions. Each time, participants immediately recognized the value of the process.

Many would eagerly take notes or snap pictures as I explained the method on a whiteboard or a flip chart. The consensus was clear: the method was grounded in common sense and proposed an excellent positive habit. Yet, despite their initial enthusiasm, the majority failed to integrate it into their lives meaningfully.

Excuses often followed: "I am too busy," or "I sat down to answer the questions but could not think of anything to write." Some even claimed they went through the process mentally just to avoid embarrassment. Over the years, one thing has become evident: people struggle to embrace this practice not because it is difficult, but because they lack clarity with their purpose, goals, and PSM. Without well-defined and documented purpose, goals, and PSM, even the simplest questions become hard to answer.

Another revealing experience came during my time as a guest lecturer at the University of Malta, working with students aged 18 to 21. While their next big goal to graduate was usually clear, they often lacked PSMs to structure their approach to reaching that goal. For example, few had quantified the number of hours they needed to dedicate to studying, resting, or socializing to maintain a balanced life during their studies. Their longer-term ambitions often revolved around vague aspirations like, "I want to own my own hospital" or, "I want to start my own business." While these dreams are admirable, they are so distant that they lack the necessary traction to guide meaningful progress. As life evolves with jobs, relationships, and family responsibilities, these long-term goals risk remaining unfulfilled, leading to frustration or a sense of emptiness.

I learned to approach this challenge differently. Like everyone else, I had and still have big dreams. But I discovered the power of breaking down those lofty ambitions into smaller, attainable goals with time frames of three to nine months. This strategy created a sense of urgency and focus, while also providing frequent opportunities to achieve and celebrate success. With each win, I gained momentum and confidence, realizing that consistent small victories were the key to reaching my larger goals.

This method of aligning minor goals with overarching dreams transformed my approach to success. Over time, the cumulative effect of these smaller wins led me to believe in the possibility of achieving my biggest ambitions. Each win reinforced my determination and built the foundation for realizing what once seemed unattainable. The lesson is simple but profound:

by structuring your goals with clear PSMs and celebrating incremental progress, you create the focus, urgency, and belief necessary to transform dreams into reality.

Personal Success Metrics (PSMs) are not just about tracking progress. They are about creating momentum, maintaining clarity, and staying committed to personal growth. When purpose, goals, and PSMs are well defined and aligned, they transform aspirations into measurable achievements and ensure that every step forward is intentional. The Thriveon Method provides a structured approach to help you reflect, adjust, and keep moving toward your best self. Success is not accidental; it is built through consistent action, self-awareness, and measurable progress. Now that you have been exposed to the Thriveon Method and PSMs, the question is no longer about understanding the process, it is about deciding. Will you embrace the moment and commit to becoming a Thriveon practitioner, or will you let hesitation hold you back?

SOMETHING TO PONDER

Measurement is about scoring yourself.
Evaluation is about improving.
Measure and evaluate.

Call to Action: This is a good time to reflect and take note of your thoughts. Below are three example PSMs.

1. **Social Media Balance**: Limit screen time on social media to two hours a day. Track your daily usage for one week to see your progress.

2. **Mental Health Check**: Practice one mindfulness activity, like meditation or journaling, for ten minutes a day. Measure how consistently you do it over the next seven days.

3. **Self-Worth Tracker**: Write down three things you like about yourself or are proud of each day. Review your list at the end of the week to reflect on your growth.

TAKE THE NEXT STEP IN YOUR JOURNEY

To truly harness **the power of PSMs**, it is essential to move beyond understanding and into action. The next step is to design your own **Personal Success Metrics (PSMs)** using the **PSM Construction Formula**, ensuring that your **PSMs** are clear, measurable, achievable and fully aligned with your goals.

This exercise is not just about PSM setting, it is about creating a **road map for personal success**. The clarity you gain will empower you to track progress, make intentional improvements, and accelerate your growth.

Before moving on to the next chapter, invest in yourself. **Your transformation starts now.**

6

THE POWER OF NOW

Growth does not wait for the perfect moment. The perfect moment is now. Too often, we delay action, waiting for the 'right time', only to find that hesitation turns into inaction, and inaction becomes regret. But what if the only thing standing between you and your transformation is your decision to start today?

You now have the tools, the Thriveon Method, the structure of PSMs, and a clear path to measurable progress. The next step is not about more preparation; it is about commitment. In this chapter, you will discover why there is no better time than now to take action, align your daily choices with your purpose, and fully embrace your journey toward becoming your best self. The moment of change is here – will you take it?

In many pubs across the United Kingdom, you might spot a sign that reads, "Free Beer Tomorrow." At first glance, it is a clever joke, a bit of humour to amuse patrons. But beneath the laughter lies a deeper truth: tomorrow never comes. The promise is an illusion, much like the way we convince ourselves that action can always wait for another day.

This humorous sign reveals a deeper truth about human nature, our habit of postponing action to a tomorrow that never arrives. It is a trap many fall into, convincing themselves that there will always be time to do what truly matters. This mindset is fuelled by inertia, the silent force that thrives in comfort zones. It whispers that delaying action is harmless, that waiting until tomorrow is just as good as starting today. But tomorrow often turns into next week, next month, or even never.

Embrace the present. The power of now is entirely in your hands. Only you can decide that this moment, not tomorrow, not next week, is the right time to act. Through my own experiences, I have learned that the most expensive cost in life is not money, it is procrastination.

Procrastination is the thief of time and opportunity. It silently kills dreams, stifles ambition and limits potential. Each moment you delay is a moment you will never get back. The past is gone, the future is uncertain, and the only time you truly control is now.

Tomorrow is an illusion. Think about all the times you have told yourself, *"I will start tomorrow."* How often has tomorrow come and gone without any change? This cycle of delay leads to missed opportunities and unfulfilled potential. The idea of starting later feels comfortable, but it is just a way to avoid discomfort and responsibility. It keeps us stuck in planning mode, endlessly preparing but never executing.

Consider the pub sign once more: "Free beer tomorrow." It is a promise that is never fulfilled because when tomorrow arrives, it becomes today, and the offer is pushed to yet another tomorrow. The same applies to waiting for the perfect moment, the perfect opportunity, or the perfect conditions. If you keep waiting, you will realize they never truly arrive.

Break free from inertia. Inertia is the force that keeps you standing still. It thrives in the comfort of routine and the fear of the unknown. It convinces you that waiting is safer than taking action. But here is the truth: waiting does not remove uncertainty; it only deepens doubt. To overcome inertia, you must cultivate a sense of urgency and a bias toward action. Recognize that waiting for tomorrow often means waiting forever. Instead of focusing on what might go wrong, shift your mindset to what you can control right now.

The true cost of procrastination. Procrastination is not just a habit; it is a silent killer of progress. Its cost is immeasurable because what it steals from you cannot be replaced.

- It costs you time, the one resource you can never get back
- It costs you opportunities, chances that may never come again
- It costs you growth, delaying the person you are meant to become.

Every moment spent waiting is a moment stolen from your future.

> From my own experience, I know how easy it is to slip into the comfort of procrastination, especially when life feels overwhelming. It is easy to think,

"I will deal with it tomorrow" or, "Things will get better on their own." But here is the hard truth: tomorrow does not fix anything. If you wait long enough, "tomorrow" becomes "never."

When I was a teenager, my home life was complicated. My parents stayed together, but they were not aligned in their values or how they approached life. For a kid, it was confusing and often painful. I did not have the stability that many of my peers seemed to enjoy, and I used that as my excuse to retreat. School felt pointless. Why work hard when I could just blame my circumstances for where I was? It was easier to sit back, wait for something to change, and let life happen to me.

I fell into a trap that I did not even realize was there: self-pity and procrastination. I told myself I was not good enough or that maybe I just was not meant for more. I started to believe I did not deserve success or fulfilment. And do you know what that got me? Nothing. No progress. No growth. Just time wasted. Looking back, those years of waiting, those years I convinced myself it was not the right time came at a steep cost. Time is the one thing you can never get back.

But here is the thing: you do not have to wait for life to change. You can decide to change it yourself. That is what I finally realized. One day, I stopped waiting for the perfect moment and accepted that it did not exist. I started to ask myself: "What small thing can I do today?" It was not easy, most worthwhile things never are, but by setting simple, consistent goals and showing up every day, I started to see progress. Bit by bit, I reclaimed my time, my confidence and my purpose.

Here is what I learned: procrastination is the most expensive thing in life. Each day you wait is a day you will never get back. Deciding not to decide is not neutral, it is a choice to stay stuck. And every day you stay stuck is a day you are giving away your future.

To anyone reading this: do not wait. Do not convince yourself that you are not ready or that the time is not right. The time is never perfect. The only time you have is now. Even the smallest step forward is better than standing still. Whether it is signing up for that course, sending the email you have been avoiding, or taking five minutes to reflect on your goals, just start.

Because here is the truth: nothing changes until you do. And when you take that first step, when you commit to showing up for yourself every day, you will find that progress feels better than perfection. You will start to see what is possible when you stop waiting and start acting.

That experience taught me a valuable lesson: the perfect time is now. There will always be excuses to wait, but the cost of waiting is far too high. Action creates momentum. You must move forward with the information and resources you have right now. Progress does not come from waiting; it comes from starting.

Take immediate action and harness the now. How? It starts with a mindset shift recognizing that your actions today define your future. The choices you make in this moment will shape the life you will live.

The following are practical steps to harness the power of now.

Set Clear Goals: Define what you want to achieve. Clarity provides both direction and motivation. Create your own PSMs to measure progress and hold yourself accountable.

Break Down Tasks: Large goals can feel overwhelming. Break them down into smaller, manageable steps you can take immediately. Focus on quick wins; they build confidence, fuel motivation, and create momentum.

Prioritize: Focus on what truly matters. Identify tasks that have the greatest impact and tackle them first. Apply the Pareto Principle (80/20 rule): 20% of your efforts will drive 80% of your fulfilment.[5] Prioritize wisely.

Eliminate Distractions: Create an environment that supports focus. Remove anything that derails progress. Self-pity is the greatest distraction. It is like a hole in a fuel tank, slowly draining your energy until nothing remains.

Take the First Step: Starting is the hardest part. Take action, no matter how small, because action breeds motivation.

Build Momentum: Once you start, keep going. Momentum is powerful; it will push you through challenges. Make your goals visible. If needed, transform your personal space into a war room with reminders, lists and progress trackers to keep you focused.

Final thoughts on "The Power of Now": Before wrapping up, I want to leave you with a few final thoughts for reflection.

> Poet Emily Dickinson once wrote, "Forever is composed of nows."[6] This profound truth reminds us that every moment we experience, every step we take, and every choice we make creates the tapestry of our lives. Our forever is not some distant, unattainable future. It is the accumulation of decisions made in the now.
>
> Think about it: how often do we scroll endlessly on social media, telling ourselves it is just taking a quick break, only to lose hours we can never get back? How many dreams have been pushed aside, waiting for the right moment to begin?

The distractions of technology, the pressure to appear perfect, and the fear of failure make the power of now feel both elusive and intimidating.

We recognize the harm of certain habits, excessive screen time, procrastination, neglecting our health. Yet many of us remain trapped in these cycles. These behaviours, often disguised as relaxation or self-care, do not restore us; they drain us. Instead of offering comfort, they create a loop that feels safe but keeps us stagnant.

The illusion of 'later': New Year's resolutions are a perfect example. They sound hopeful, like declarations of positive change. But in many cases, they are just a way to delay action. Saying, "I will start next year" offers temporary relief from discomfort, but true change does not happen someday, it happens the moment you begin.

Here is the truth: the only time you have control over is right now.

Be brave. Take small steps. Big changes do not start with massive leaps; they begin with the courage to move forward one moment at a time.

A modern example: breaking free from doom-scrolling. We all know how addictive doom-scrolling can be. What starts as "just five minutes" turns into an hour of mindless consumption. The idea of quitting social media entirely feels overwhelming, an impossible commitment to maintain. But what if, instead of swearing off it forever, you simply put your phone down for ten minutes? Then an hour? That small shift could mean the difference between losing time and using time. Over time, these short breaks add up, transforming distraction into focus, and lost time into meaningful progress.

The true cost of procrastination: progress is not about forever; it is about now. Every small decision lays a brick in the foundation of your best life. Over time, what once felt impossible becomes second nature.

Every choice to act now or to postpone comes at a cost. Action requires effort, discipline, and discomfort. Delay offers the illusion of ease, but its hidden price is far greater. The price is the slow erosion of potential, missed opportunities, and regrets taking root.

Consider the compounding effect. An extra hour of scrolling today? Multiply it by seven days, a month, a year. How much of your precious time could have been spent learning a skill, building relationships, or making progress toward a goal? Now, imagine the ripple effect of small efforts made today – writing the first paragraph of your blog, taking a 15-minute walk, sending the message you have been avoiding. That is how progress begins: with small, courageous actions, in the moment.

Your now is waiting for you. Dickinson's words hold even greater meaning in our age of distractions: "Forever is composed of nows." The choices you make today, letting go of unproductive habits, pursuing a long-held dream, showing yourself kindness, will ripple into your future. Each now carries the power to shape your forever.

So, as you think about the decisions you have postponed, ask yourself: "What is the cost of acting now compared to the cost of not acting?"

When you weigh those costs, the truth is undeniable: choosing to act now is not just an investment in this moment; it is an investment in your future self.

The answer does not lie in tomorrow. It is here, in this moment, waiting for you to choose it.

I do not know about you, but I believe we are all born perfectly free from fear, doubt, and limitation. We enter the world with no agenda, wrapped in complete innocence.

But as we grow, the world around us begins shaping us, introducing expectations, fears, and self-doubt. Over time, our innocence fades and we become imperfect human beings, moulded by experiences, beliefs and societal pressures.

Given this reality, the only path forward is to embrace your imperfection. One of the main reasons people procrastinate is fear of imperfection. We wait for the perfect conditions, the perfect plan, the perfect moment, but perfection is an illusion. Progress is what truly matters. Taking imperfect action is always better than taking no action at all.

Living in the now does not mean ignoring the future or failing to plan. It means taking decisive action today to create the future you desire. It means valuing your time, making the most of each moment and understanding that the only time you truly have is now, so use it wisely.

Remember, the "Free Beer Tomorrow" sign in the pub is a joke, but the lesson it teaches is serious. Do not wait for tomorrow to live your best life. Start now. The power to change is in your hands.

The Power of Now and Your Purpose. The power of now is transformative, but only if your actions are driven by something deeper. It is not just about doing more or moving faster; it is about moving with intention. Without a clear purpose, even the most disciplined action can feel empty.

This is where many people struggle. They set goals, make plans, and even take action, but without a strong 'why,' motivation fades and procrastination takes over. The Thriveon Method is only truly effective when your actions are aligned with your purpose (why), your goals (what), and your PSM (how). Because action without direction is movement without meaning.

To break free from procrastination, you must first define your purpose. Why do you want to grow? What is driving you forward? What is the greater vision that fuels your ambition? Clarity of purpose transforms effort into fulfillment.

You have now reached a pivotal moment. The moment where knowledge turns into action. You understand the Thriveon Method, you recognize the importance of PSMs, and you see the power of taking control of your journey. But none of it matters unless you make the choice to begin. Becoming a Thriveon practitioner is not just a commitment to self-improvement, it is a decision to show up for yourself every day, to embrace growth with purpose and to track your progress with intention.

The time for action is now.

The first step in this journey is to understand your purpose. Because, before you can define your goals and measure progress, you must first grasp why you are on this path. In the next chapter, Purpose in Life, we will take a deep dive into the foundation of meaningful growth.

SOMETHING TO PONDER

Your ***excuses*** are ***seducers***.
Your ***fears*** are ***liars***.
Your ***doubts*** are ***thieves***.

Call to Action: This is a good time to reflect and take note of your thoughts.

1. **Stop the Wait**: What is one thing you have been putting off? Do it today; start small but start now.

2. **Set Your Focus**: Write one clear goal you want to crush this week; make it simple, make it happen.

3. **Cut the Noise**: Eliminate distraction. Turn off notifications for one hour a day to stay focused. Start right now.

TAKE THE NEXT STEP IN YOUR JOURNEY

To truly embrace **the Power of Now**, you must move beyond intention and into **immediate action**. The next step is to break free from hesitation and take **concrete steps today** toward your goals.

This exercise is not just about identifying what you want, it is about **taking real, tangible steps forward, right now**. The momentum you create today will set the stage for lasting success, helping you overcome procrastination and build habits of continuous progress.

Before moving on to the next chapter, commit to action. **Your future begins with what you do now.**

7

PURPOSE IN LIFE

Every journey starts with a destination in mind. But how do you choose the right path if you do not know where you are meant to go?

Many people set goals, chase achievements, and seek success only to realize that something is missing. That missing element is purpose. A clear sense of purpose gives your life meaning and direction.

Your purpose is your 'why.' It is the force that drives you, the deeper reason behind your ambitions, and the compass that keeps you on course. Purpose is the core driver of motivation and fulfilment. Without it, growth and goals lack focus, they become empty checkboxes, and achievements can feel meaningless. But when your actions align with your purpose, every step forward becomes fulfilling, intentional, and deeply rewarding.

In this chapter, we will explore how to define your purpose, why it is essential for personal success, and how it serves as the foundation for setting your goals and structuring your PSMs. Because once you understand your why, your what and how become infinitely clearer.

What is your purpose in life? Have your ever asked yourself this question?

This question is deceptively simple but strikes at the very heart of human existence. For centuries, individuals have sought to define their reason for being, and yet, for many, the answer remains elusive.

While many search for one singular purpose, the reality is that each of us can hold multiple purposes across different areas of our lives. Just as life is multi-dimensional, so too is purpose. You may find distinct purposes in your career, relationships, health, personal growth, financial wellbeing, spirituality, or contribution to others. Each focus area can carry its own 'why,' with unique goals, and each goal supported by one or more Personal Success Metrics (PSMs).

It is neither practical nor necessary to try and optimize every area all at once. Instead, focus on the areas that offer the greatest value and relevance to you based on where you are in life. A young adult might prioritize career and financial freedom, while someone later in life may find greater purpose in contribution or creativity. The beauty of purpose is that it evolves with you and recognizing that you can have more than one purpose allows you to live with both clarity and balance.

A study conducted by the Cultural Research Centre at Arizona Christian University revealed staggering insights into this modern struggle.[7] According to the findings, three-fourths (75%) of Millennials, those born between 1981 and 1996, are desperately seeking meaning and purpose in life, making them the most likely among adults to question their reason for living. Deep yearning is evident, as 95% of Millennials feel that their lives require significant changes.

This generational crisis extends far beyond Millennials. Among older generations, fewer than one in five adults (22%) view life as sacred, and half believe that "life is what you make it," devoid of any absolute value. The lack of clarity about purpose in life often leads to frustration, dissatisfaction, and even despair. As CRC (Cultural Research Centre) Director of Research George Barna notes, "Tens of millions of young adults are stuck at the starting gate of adult life, unable to find direction."

These statistics paint a sobering picture, but they also illuminate an opportunity, a chance to redefine how we approach the question of purpose. Purpose is not just a philosophical exercise; it is a practical tool that shapes our decisions, guides our values, and brings fulfilment to our lives.

At its core, purpose gives meaning to the mundane. It transforms everyday actions into deliberate steps toward a larger goal. And yet, purpose cannot be handed down or borrowed; it must be discovered through reflection and action.

This chapter invites you to explore your unique purpose. Through stories, insights, and the structured Thriveon Method, you will uncover ways to align your daily actions with the values and goals that define your life's meaning. In the process, you will gain the clarity and confidence to move forward with intention, making your journey one of fulfilment and growth. The search for purpose is not a luxury; it is a necessity.

Purpose is more than a goal or a milestone; it is the very essence that drives us, fuels our passion and brings fulfilment to our existence. When we align our actions with a deep sense of purpose, we find ourselves enriched with energy, motivation, and a sense of belonging that transcends the material rewards of work and daily life.

Imagine being so connected to what you are doing that, even late into the night, you feel compelled to keep going, not out of obligation, but out of an unrelenting drive that brings joy, satisfaction, and meaning. This is the power of purpose. It is what elevates a task from a chore to a calling, making even the mundane feel significant.

From my own experience, purpose can change everything. In my early days working in information technology, I led a small team of software developers, focusing on business and systems analysis. One project took me to the main hospital in Malta, where I spent weeks building systems to streamline patient services. It was there that I met Mary (the name does not refer to the real person in the story), a woman who would unknowingly teach me a powerful lesson.

Mary was in her late 40s, stationed at a small desk at the end of a corridor, her daily routine unwavering. From eight in the morning until four in the afternoon, Monday through Friday, she sat, sorting piles of thick, three-ply prescription forms. Each day, she methodically separated the white, pink, and yellow sheets, stacking them into precise piles. Her appearance reflected her state of mind: muted and unassuming. She wore loose, functional clothing, her hair tied back in a way that spoke of practicality rather than care. Her face told a story of fatigue, a quiet resignation softened by a sense of duty. She was there because she needed the security of a pay cheque, a stability her family depended on.

On my third day, curiosity got the better of me. Her desk was strategically positioned, possibly to help with directing people through the maze of corridors, and I stopped for a quick chat. I asked her, "Why are you separating the forms? Why the colours: white, pink, and yellow?"

She looked at me, a bit surprised by the question, and replied with a shrug, "I do not really know. I have never thought much about it. It is just what they told me to do."

Something about her tone and the weary look in her eyes struck me. "How long have you been doing this?" I asked.

Her shoulders slumped slightly as she sighed. "Five long years," she said, her voice tinged with both weariness and the faintest hint of something deeper, perhaps disappointment in herself or the situation.

I walked away, but I could not shake the thought of her, day after day, sitting at that desk without understanding why her work mattered. It seemed such a small act, sorting paper, monotonous, even mind-numbing. But was it truly meaningless?

Determined to find an answer, I began asking around, speaking with the administrative staff, nurses and even doctors. Gradually, I uncovered the truth: Mary's seemingly simple task was far from trivial. Those carefully separated sheets were the start of a process that ensured discharged and outpatient individuals received their prescriptions on time. Without her, patients would wait longer, treatment schedules would falter, and the efficiency of the hospital would suffer. Mary's work, quiet and humble, was a vital thread in the fabric of patient care.

I hurried back down the corridor to her desk, eager to share what I had learned. "Mary," I said, lowering my voice slightly as if to convey the gravity of my words, "do you know that because of you, patients receive their medication on time, every time? Your work is essential to their recovery and wellbeing."

Her face lit up with surprise, her eyes widening as she absorbed my words. Her hand instinctively went to her chest, as though steadying herself against the weight of the revelation. "Is that right?" she asked, a tentative smile beginning to form.

"Yes," I replied. "Thanks to your dedication and attention to detail, patients leave the hospital with everything they need to heal. You are not just sorting papers; you are making a real difference in people's lives. You are a hero, Mary. Because of you, people are getting a better chance at a healthy recovery."

In that moment, Mary's eyes welled up with tears. For a brief second, she looked down at her desk, her hands resting on the piles of paper that had once seemed so insignificant. Then she looked back up at me, her expression a mix of disbelief and newfound pride. She had come in touch with something far beyond the task of sorting papers; she had glimpsed her purpose. Knowing that her work was meaningful, that it impacted lives, had unlocked a new energy in her. She understood her value, her contribution. That simple awareness transformed her routine, fueling her with a renewed commitment. She was no longer just sorting papers; she was enabling healing and care.

From then on, Mary's approach to her work changed. The task was the same, but now it had purpose. She began arriving at her desk with a spring in her step. Her clothing became brighter, more polished, as though reflecting the lightness she now felt inside. She set small goals, aiming to process even more forms each day, motivated by the knowledge that her efforts made a real difference. Even her colleagues noticed the shift, remarking on how her smile now lit up the otherwise sterile corridors of the hospital.

Purpose is powerful. When we understand our purpose, we connect with our value. We see meaning in our actions and, with it, the desire to grow. Mary's story is a reminder that when we recognize our purpose, even the smallest tasks can become steps toward a greater mission.

Purpose in What You Do. Beyond survival and security, purpose is essential in any environment where we invest significant time and mental energy. Whether at work, university, or within an organization, team, or community. Many people find themselves at various stages within Maslow's Hierarchy of Needs, ranging from 'Survival,' where they work purely for financial stability or necessities, to 'Security,' where they seek consistency, benefits, or predictability.[8] However, moving beyond these levels requires more than just getting by. It involves finding belonging, feeling important and, ultimately, self-actualization in what we do.

For those at the base of the hierarchy, purpose may seem distant. When the primary focus is on survival, whether earning a wage, passing exams, or meeting basic obligations, there is little room for self-reflection or deeper aspirations. Yet, even in these situations, purpose can be found in small ways. A person in a survival-focused job might take pride in the quality of their work. A student struggling with coursework might find motivation in mastering a subject or learning something meaningful. An individual in an organization might derive satisfaction from simply being part of a larger process that contributes to something greater.

As individuals progress toward 'Belonging' and 'Importance,' purpose becomes increasingly attainable. In the Belonging stage, people feel connected to something bigger, their values align with their workplace, institution, or organization, and they contribute to a shared mission. This connection fosters deeper engagement and personal satisfaction. Beyond belonging lies 'Importance,' where individuals do not just fit within a system, they see themselves as vital to it. They recognize their unique contributions, leading to a greater sense of pride, fulfillment, and accomplishment.

At the highest level lies Self-Actualization where engagement is no longer just about external validation; it becomes an expression of one's values, talents and vision. At this stage, purpose is not something to be discovered, it is lived. Whether in a career, a university setting or a community, self-actualized individuals find meaning in what they do, inspiring those around them and making a meaningful impact in their field or environment.

Wherever you are today, whether working, studying, or contributing to a greater cause, purpose is within reach. By recognizing where you stand and striving to move forward, you open the door to deeper fulfillment, engagement and success in whatever path you pursue.

Another experience I have been privileged to be privy to is my time with Brian (the name Brian does not refer to the real person in the story). After closing the chapter on my IT company, I ventured into business consultancy, a move that introduced me to clients outside the tech sphere. From supermarkets to tourism, logistics to real estate, I found myself learning from remarkable individuals across diverse industries.

Some years ago, I met Brian, a young man in his early 30s who had navigated some of life's roughest waters. A history of substance addiction had led him to the brink of death after an overdose, a stint in prison, and a long but successful rehabilitation program. Emerging from the shadows of his past, Brian was determined to rebuild his life. He found a position at a real estate company that offered him a fresh start, albeit with no fixed income. His success hinged entirely on his ability to earn commissions.

Yet, rebuilding was not as simple as earning money. It was about earning back something far more fragile: his own self-esteem and the trust of those he loved. The company, to its credit, provided Brian with extensive training, mentorship and tools to succeed. This is where our paths crossed, and I count myself lucky to have witnessed Brian's transformation firsthand.

Brian's Struggle with Identity. In our early one-on-one coaching sessions, I asked Brian what he saw when he looked in the mirror. His response was filled with gratitude but tinged with resignation: "I see a survivor, someone trying hard but always under judgment. I see a man thankful for a second chance, but still uncertain if he deserves it."

Despite showing promise, Brian was weighed down by social judgment and the belief that his work lacked meaning. Every client interaction felt like a silent judgment, each handshake a test of his worthiness. Yet, he pressed on, not just for himself but to prove to his loved ones that he was genuinely changing. As he started listing properties, selling homes and reaping the financial rewards, we introduced PSMs to structure his growth.

Weekly goals like the number of properties listed, social media campaigns launched and client calls made helped him achieve consistent results. Within nine months, Brian had transitioned from surviving to thriving.

The Missing Purpose. At the end of Brian's first year, we met for a review. I asked him again, "When you look in the mirror now, who do you see?" He replied, "I see someone who has earned a second chance but is still ... just a salesman."

His words, his tone, and his posture told me that Brian was excelling materially but lacked a sense of purpose. He did not see the deeper impact of his work.

I remembered Mary's transformation, and I knew Brian needed a similar revelation. I said, "Brian, you are not just a salesman. You are a guide, a healer, a transformer of lives."

Brian looked at me sceptically, his forehead furrowing as if unsure whether to believe me. But I pressed on.

Revealing Brian's Purpose. "Think about it," I said. "When you help a young couple buy their first home, you are doing more than selling property. You are giving them a foundation for their dreams, a space to create memories, and a place to call their own. You are shaping their future."

I continued, "And when you help an elderly widow sell her property so she can afford a care home, you are not simply closing a sale. You are giving her the gift of security, comfort, and the dignity to face her final years with peace of mind. Brian, your work transforms lives, just as others transformed yours when you needed it most."

As I spoke, I saw a shift in Brian's demeanour. His eyes, once clouded with doubt, began to clear. His shoulders, which carried the weight of his past, relaxed slightly. A spark of recognition lit up his face. He understood. His role was no longer about selling properties; it was about being a catalyst for change, a symbol of hope.

Brian's New Purpose. Once Brian embraced this purpose, he added new KPIs to reflect his mission. For instance, he began actively sourcing affordable properties for first-time buyers, determined to make a difference for young couples starting their lives. He started taking extra time with clients, listening to their stories and offering solutions tailored to their unique situations. With every sale, he saw not just a transaction, but a life changed. Brian's work became a reflection of his own journey, a story of hope, transformation and purpose. His renewed sense of self even began to show in small but meaningful ways. His smile came more easily, his confidence grew, and he no longer hesitated to make eye contact. He was not hiding anymore.

Through this newfound understanding, Brian's trajectory changed. His purpose ignited his passion, and his passion fuelled his success.

Brian's story, like Mary's, is a testament to the power of finding meaning in our lives. When we align our actions with a higher purpose, we do not just elevate ourselves, we elevate everyone we touch.

Purpose and the Journey of Self-Actualization: Self-actualization is a journey, not a destination. It requires continuous self-reflection, learning, and a commitment to growth. The Thriveon Method provides a structured approach to help you navigate this journey by encouraging you to ask the hard questions:

- *What drives me?*
- *Where do I find my purpose in different areas of my life?*
- *How can I align my daily actions with my deepest values?*

By regularly assessing your PSMs, your personal signposts across wellbeing, physical health, personal development, career, and other meaningful areas, you can track progress, recognize achievements, and adjust to ensure your actions remain aligned with your purpose.

Constructing Your Purpose Statement. Purpose is not singular; it evolves with context. At any given time, you may wear multiple hats: a university student, a professional, a volunteer in an organization. Each role may have a different purpose, and it is important to define your purpose in the specific area of life you are focusing on.

To craft your Purpose Statement, reflect on the following:

1. **Values**: What are the core principles that guide your decisions? What do you stand for? Your purpose must align with these.

2. **Passion**: What excites you? What activities make you feel alive and fulfilled? Your purpose should be rooted in what you love doing.

3. **Contribution**: How do you want to make a difference? How will your purpose impact your workplace, community, or personal life?

The Purpose Statement Construction Formula:

Purpose Statement = 1 [**Verb**] + "to" + [**Contribution**] + "by using my passion" + [**Passions**] + "while honouring my core" + [**Values**].

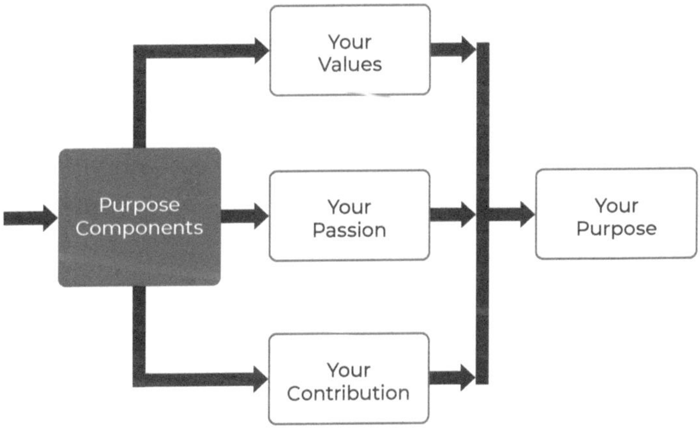

To begin crafting your Purpose Statement, ask yourself:

- *What impact do I want to leave on the world around me?*
- *What legacy do I want to leave behind me in this job, university, or organization?*
- *How do my strengths align with my passions?*

Your Purpose Statement should be clear, intentional, and deeply personal. It should guide you like a compass, ensuring that your daily efforts contribute to a bigger picture.

Take Action, Define Your Purpose. Now, take a moment to pause and reflect. Choose one focus area of your life, be it work, education, community involvement or personal development and craft your Purpose Statement. Here are three examples to guide you:

- As a university student: *"I dedicate myself to advancing society by using my passion for learning and critical thinking while honouring my core values of curiosity, integrity, and service."*
- As a professional in a leadership role: *"I devote my leadership to empowering my team to achieve excellence by using my passion for coaching and growth while honouring my core values of trust, collaboration, and resilience."*
- As a member of an environmental organization: *"I strive to promote environmental stewardship by using my passion for sustainability and conservation while honouring my core values of responsibility, compassion, and community."*

Your Purpose Statement is a living statement, it may evolve as you grow. What matters is that it gives you direction, clarity, and a sense of fulfillment.

Once you define your Purpose Statement (your why), the next step is to define your goals (your what – destination) followed by the definition of your PSMs (your how – sign-posts). The following model outlines the model that will lead you to create your personal growth plan in line with your purpose.

Step	**Method**	**Example**
Choose Your Focus Area	Example: Personal Development, Wellbeing, Career Professional Growth, Physical Health Fitness, Nutrition Dietary Habits, Relationship Social Growth, etc.	Personal Development
Define Your Purpose (WHY?)	Purpose Statement Construction Formula: I [**Verb**] to [**Contribution**] by using my passion [**Passions**] while honouring my core [**Values**].	I **commit** to **inspiring** others to unlock their potential by using my passion for **learning** and **mentorship** while honouring my core values of **growth**, **integrity**, and **curiosity**.
Define Your Goals (WHAT?)	Goals Statement Construction Formula: [**Verb**] + [**Achievement**] + [**Specific Outcomes**] + [**By When**].	**Complete** a certified personal **development coaching** course and **deliver three free workshops** by **30 September 20XX**.
Define Your PSMs (HOW?)	PSMs Statement Construction Formula: [**Verb**] + [**Action**] + [**Target**] + [**By When**].	**Study course material for one hour every weekday morning before 8 am.**

Looking Ahead, Life's Challenges and the Corners You Will Face. A life filled with purpose is rewarding but not without obstacles. The moment you commit to growth, you will face challenges, setbacks, and moments of doubt. No one can go through life without peaks and troughs, without being pushed into difficult corners.

The next chapter explores exactly that, the inevitable challenges that shape us. How do we navigate life's corners with resilience? How do we emerge stronger?

Let's continue the journey.

SOMETHING TO PONDER

Walking into the very things that **scare** you is how you reclaim your **forgotten power.**

Fear holds many people back. Not because they are incapable, but because they hesitate to step into the unknown. Growth demands courage. Purpose is not something we stumble upon; it is something we actively shape by confronting our doubts, embracing challenges, and stepping forward with intention.

Call to Action: This is a good time to reflect and take note of your thoughts.

1. **Know Your Place**: Where are you right now in your journey? Are you merely surviving or are you thriving? Take stock of your family, friendships, work, studies and the communities you belong to. Write down what feels aligned and what feels lacking.

2. **Take the Next Step**: Progress happens one step at a time. What is one action you can take this week to move closer to fulfilment? Maybe it is learning a new skill, reaching out to someone who inspires you or setting a personal challenge. Choose one and commit to it.

3. **Define Your Why**: What excites you, energizes you, and gives you meaning? Purpose is found in action, not just thought. Identify one thing that sparks passion in you and decide one concrete way to explore it further, whether it is through study, practice, or contribution.

TAKE THE NEXT STEP IN YOUR JOURNEY

To truly embrace **your purpose in life**, you must move beyond reflection and into **intentional planning**. The next step is to create your **Personal Growth Plan**, ensuring that your **Purpose, Goals, and Personal Success Metrics (PSMs)** are clearly defined and actionable.

This exercise is not just about defining your purpose, it is about **building a road map for your best self**. The clarity you gain will empower you to align your values, set meaningful goals, and take the right actions toward lasting transformation.

Before moving on to the next chapter, commit to this process. **Your future is shaped by the purpose you define today.**

8

CORNERS

Life is a journey marked by challenges, breakthroughs, and moments of reflection. Coming from the chapter on Purpose in Life, you now understand the importance of having a clear direction, rooted in your values, passions, and contributions.

But what happens when life does not follow your plan? What happens when you encounter a corner, a moment when you feel stuck, uncertain, or overwhelmed by adversity?

These corners are inevitable. They appear as obstacles in your path, testing not only your resilience but also your commitment to your purpose. At first, they may seem insurmountable places of discomfort, doubt, or even despair. Yet, what if these corners are more than obstacles? What if they are opportunities disguised as challenges, calling on you to rise above fear, grow in strength, and reassess your direction?

Corners are checkpoints. They force you to pause, confront your vulnerabilities, and recalibrate your approach. These moments are not meant to break you; they are meant to shape you. With honesty and courage, corners become lessons in resilience, teaching you how to adapt, reflect, and forge ahead with renewed confidence and clarity.

As you navigate this chapter, embrace the truth that challenges are opportunities for growth. Life's tests are designed to strengthen your resolve and prepare you for greater heights. Resilience comes not from avoiding adversity but from facing it, learning from it, and emerging stronger. Each corner offers a lesson, an invitation to grow in wisdom, courage and purpose.

With your purpose as your guide, let's explore how to navigate the corners of life with clarity, strength, and unwavering commitment to your journey.

> **From my own experience**. As expected at my age, one would assume I have faced a few of life's corners. I am sharing here what I consider to be one of my most challenging professional corners yet.
>
> When I founded my company, 6PM, in 2001, the goal was simple but ambitious: to grow a small IT business into a force of innovation. In 2007, we achieved a significant milestone by listing 6PM on the Malta Stock Exchange, a move that filled our team with pride and hope. As part of the expansion, the board appointed a new chief executive officer, a senior British leader with experience in our main market, the United Kingdom. I took on the role of chief technical officer, confident that together we could grow the company further. But by 2009, as the global economy took a steep dive, we, like many others, felt the tremors of an impending collapse.

Then, in early 2010, a phone call came at dawn that I would never forget. The CEO and our British chairman called me from the UK, their voices tense as they explained that we had lost millions in revenue due to cancelled contracts, tightening our lifeline as a business. They presented a cold conclusion: we had to wind down the company. For them, it was business; for me, it was my life's work, my commitment to every shareholder, every team member, every family that depended on 6PM. Winding down the company would mean failure on Malta's stock exchange, making us the first company in the nation to close under such circumstances. In Malta, where communities are tightly woven and reputations carry weight, this would follow me for the rest of my life. It was not just a setback; for me, it was a defining crossroad.

I faced a choice: I could go along with the decision to close, allowing the company to fold and risk the impact on everyone involved. Or I could take a different kind of route, one that meant a fight. I could ask them to step down, take on the role of CEO, and do everything within my power to keep us afloat. This second path would mean embracing an uncertain, exhausting battle to restructure and reinvent the business, raise capital, and fight for every client, every contract, every job.

The easier corner, of course, would have been to let it go. But easy was never my purpose, and it was not going to save us. My purpose, I knew, was to rise to these difficult moments, to stand firm when things seemed impossible. So, I chose the harder path. I asked the CEO and chairman to resign, and I stepped into the role with a resolve to lead. Overnight, I took responsibility for not only the business, but the hundreds of livelihoods intertwined with it. This was no longer just about survival; it was about setting a new course, redefining our identity and transforming 6PM from the ground up. I must take this moment to thank two dear friends, Peter Bugeja and Steve Wightman, who stood by my side throughout the process through which we reinvented the 6PM business model.

For three years, I navigated through relentless obstacles, reinventing the business model, raising fresh capital, and building our first product to launch into the market. Each day was a test of endurance, requiring sharp focus, strict discipline, and a fierce commitment to my purpose. Through this, I re-affirmed the value of self-reflection. Every day, I dedicated 20 to 30 minutes to revisit the choices I had made and the challenges I had overcome, a daily ritual that became one of the secrets of my success.

> With each day, I faced my corner, digging deeper and growing stronger. In 2017, we sold the business, securing a win for our investors, our team, and for myself.
>
> That corner saw me through the transition from survival to self-actualization. It taught me that every corner in life is an invitation to grow and transform, no matter how daunting it seems. Embrace your corners, they are life's greatest teachers, guiding you toward resilience, purpose and, ultimately, toward a life you can look back on with pride.

In this chapter, we will explore the paradox of the corner, a space that feels confining and overwhelming yet holds the potential to unlock your greatest growth and liberation.

Life rarely offers warnings about the corners that will test your very core. These moments arrive unannounced, disrupting the comfort of routine and shaking the foundation of who you believe you are. They bring pain, doubt, and vulnerability, leaving you uncertain of your ability to endure. Yet, within these corners lies an undeniable truth: while they may momentarily break you, they also awaken within you a resilience and strength you never imagined is possible.

Corners are not just places of struggle; they are crucibles of transformation. They challenge you to face yourself with honesty, to rise despite the odds, and to emerge stronger, wiser, and more aligned with your purpose.

More corners, from my own experience. I was 27 when I hit not one, but two of the hardest corners of my life. First, the betrayal. It was a Monday morning when someone I trusted deeply pulled the rug out from under me, shattering my confidence and leaving me questioning everything. For weeks, I spiralled. It was not sadness, it was something heavier, darker. A helplessness so consuming that even the thought of standing up, of doing something, anything, felt impossible. I was not in a comfort zone or a fear zone. I was in what I call the helpless zone, a place so void of light that even anger or self-pity seemed like luxuries.

Then, one week later, a second corner. My father fell from a height of over 12 meters in a freak accident, landing in a coma with doctors giving him just days to live. That Monday evening, I sat in a sterile hospital room, told that the only thing I could do was pray. The two pillars of my life, trust in a close friend and the security of my father's strength were gone in the span of seven days. The weight of it was unbearable.

> But here is what I could not see then: corner two, as cruel as it was, saved me. My father's accident, his fight for survival, became my purpose when I had none. Every hour spent at his bedside, every prayer whispered, was a reminder that I was still here. I still had something to give. The love I poured into him began to rebuild the worth that corner one had stolen. I did not realize it at the time, but corner two distracted me from the pain of corner one, preventing me from making reckless, impulsive decisions that could have worsened my descent.
>
> It took two years to crawl out of those corners. Corner one eventually revealed itself as a blessing, though not in the way I expected. That betrayal forced me onto a path I never would have chosen, a path that led to the kind of happiness and fulfilment I had never imagined. Corner two taught me about miracles, not just in the way my father defied the odds, waking up and walking out of the hospital in a suit, but in the way faith, love and resilience can rebuild a shattered soul.

Corners will come for you. They will arrive uninvited, stripping away your certainties and forcing you to confront the raw, unfiltered truth of your life. They will challenge you in ways you never thought possible, making you question your strength, your direction and even your worth. But within these moments of pain and uncertainty lie life's most profound lessons.

Corners teach patience because healing is not instantaneous. It is a process, slow, and often gruelling, but one that reshapes you in the waiting. They teach self-love, because even in your lowest moments, when the world feels unbearable, you are still deserving of care, compassion and forgiveness. And they teach faith, faith in time, in your ability to endure and in the promise of light, even when the darkness feels endless.

Corners will both break you and make you. They strip away the parts of you that no longer serve your growth, clearing the way for something stronger, wiser, and more resilient to emerge. They are not just moments of pain, they are invitations to rebuild, to transform, and to discover the depths of your strength.

If you are in a corner now, know this: you are not alone, and you are not stuck. Trust in the process. Trust in time. Even if the way out is not clear now, believe that it exists. When you emerge, and you will, you will carry with you a strength you never knew you possessed, a wisdom forged through struggle, and a renewed sense of purpose.

You will thrive on, not despite your corners, but because of them.

Again, from experience. Working with young people has led me to witness individuals suffering from FOMO – the Fear of Missing Out. For many young people, FOMO is indeed a corner. Overcoming FOMO is key and truly important for one's growth.

FOMO is a concept that often creates unnecessary stress and anxiety for those who fall prey to its pull. It is a powerful mindset rooted in a desire to connect, to belong and to be part of meaningful experiences. While the drive to connect is inherently positive, left unchecked, FOMO can cloud judgment, disrupt priorities, and lead to feelings of inadequacy.

The key to overcoming FOMO is to shift your focus from what you might miss to what truly matters to you.

The Root of FOMO: Connection vs. Pressure. At its core, FOMO stems from the innate human need to connect. Networking, bonding with friends, and being part of vibrant experiences are undoubtedly enriching, but when this need becomes a source of anxiety, it is time to pause and reflect.

Imagine a typical summer evening when multiple events overlap. A concert featuring an artist you admire coincides with a close friend's dinner party. It is easy to spiral into the mental gymnastics of trying to attend both or worrying about what you will miss at the event you do not attend. But here is the truth: trying to do it all often results in stress that robs you of the very joy these experiences are meant to bring.

If you experience this corner, this is how to approach FOMO positively. Rather than letting FOMO dictate your choices, adopt a mindset that focuses on intentionality and alignment with your goals and values. Here is how:

1. **Evaluate the Value of Each Opportunity**: Ask yourself:
    - Is the concert a rare opportunity to see an artist you may never experience again?
    - Is the dinner party a milestone event, like a close friend's birthday or a farewell celebration?
    - Which event aligns better with your current goals or brings greater personal fulfilment?

    By weighing the significance of each event, you can make a thoughtful choice that reflects what truly matters to you, rather than being consumed by the fear of what you are missing.

2. **Prioritize Without Guilt**. Accept that you cannot be everywhere at once. This acceptance is not a limitation but a form of empowerment. Choosing one event over another does not diminish your value or relationships, it simply means you have chosen to honour what feels most meaningful to you in that moment.

3. **Avoid Comparison and Comfort-Driven Decisions**. Let your decision be guided by what resonates with you, not by where you will feel less judged or more fitting. Choosing an event solely because it is easier or because you fear judgment from one group can perpetuate the very anxiety FOMO thrives on. Instead, focus on what aligns with your personal goals and brings you genuine joy or growth.

A Balanced Perspective on FOMO. FOMO is a complex psychological phenomenon, a mix of cognitive, behavioural, and even addictive tendencies. It creates a false urgency, making you feel like missing out on one experience will somehow diminish your happiness or success. This simply is not true.

In my own life, balancing a dynamic career, diverse hobbies, and a busy social calendar often means navigating overlapping invitations.

My wife and I, together or individually, frequently face the challenge of choosing between events. Over time, I have learned that prioritizing is not about saying “no” to people, it is about saying “yes” to what matters most.

When you approach these choices with clarity, you free yourself from the grip of FOMO and make space for experiences that enrich your life.

The Takeaway. Turning FOMO Into JOMO (Joy of Missing Out). The next time you face conflicting opportunities, remember that you hold the power to choose what aligns best with your goals and values.

- Embrace the fact that you cannot do it all, and that is okay.
- Prioritize experiences that matter most to you.
- Focus on the joy and fulfilment that come from your chosen path, rather than dwelling on what you did not choose.

By reframing FOMO as an opportunity to focus on what is meaningful, you transform it from a source of stress into a tool for living with intention and purpose.

Understanding the Corner. Life will inevitably push you into corners; unexpected spaces where options feel limited, and challenges seem overwhelming. These tight and testing moments strip away the familiar comforts of routine, leaving you exposed and vulnerable. Yet, corners are often life's most effective teachers. They do not just test your resilience; they build it. Here is what they taught me:

Corners Strip Away Comfort. Corners pull you out of your comfort zone, forcing you to confront the unexpected and adapt to situations beyond your control. It is not about being unshaken, it is about learning to steady yourself despite the chaos. The process of adaptation builds resilience, teaching you to find strength in uncertainty.

Corners Demand Self-Awareness. When life pushes you into a corner, you are often left with your rawest emotions: fear, confusion, anger, or doubt. These moments strip away distractions, leaving you face-to-face with yourself. This forced self-reflection is an opportunity to uncover your core values, discover what truly matters, and anchor yourself in your inner strength.

Corners Teach You to Trust Time. Not every corner has an immediate solution. Resilience grows when you learn to give time its due.

Understand that healing, growth, and clarity often unfold gradually. Trusting the process does not mean inaction; it means enduring the discomfort, one step at a time, and believing that progress is happening even when it is not visible.

Corners Foster Creativity and Resourcefulness. When familiar exits are blocked, corners force you to think differently. They challenge you to focus on what you can control and to utilize the resources at your disposal. This resourcefulness, cultivated under pressure, becomes a cornerstone of resilience, enabling you to find unexpected solutions in the most unlikely places.

Corners Build a New Perspective. Emerging from a corner gives you a fresh perspective. Surviving one challenge makes the next one less daunting and, over time, you come to see corners not as threats but as opportunities for growth. This mindset shift is a hallmark of resilient individuals.

Corners Reveal the Power of Connection. Some corners teach you that resilience is not a solo act. They reveal the importance of leaning on others for support, whether it is a friend, a mentor or even a stranger. Seeking and accepting help is a strength, not a weakness, and it builds the kind of interconnected resilience that strengthens everyone involved.

> **Corners Give Meaning to the Struggle**. Resilience is born when you attach meaning to your struggles. Corners invite you to ask, "What can this teach me?" or "How can this transform me?" Answering these questions turns hardship into purpose, making every challenge a stepping-stone toward growth.

Corners are life's uninvited teachers, forcing you into an accelerated course in resilience. They do not just show you how strong you are; they make you stronger. Resilience is not about avoiding hardship but about learning to weather it, and corners, painful as they might be, are the forge where that strength is born.

The key is to emerge not just intact but transformed, carrying with you the deep knowledge that, while life can corner you, it cannot confine you.

Many individuals, when faced with such corners, react with urgency, attempting to escape at any cost. They may resort to shortcuts, betray their values or blame external circumstances. Driven by pride, they avoid discomfort and seek the quickest way out, even if it means compromising integrity.

Others, however, have learned that corners are not curses but opportunities. They recognize that life's challenges are often stepping-stones, cloaked in difficulty but designed for growth. Embracing a corner means practicing self-reflection, setting intentional PSMs and remaining accountable to oneself. It means resisting the urge to escape and, instead, leaning into the lessons that discomfort can teach.

Who are you? One to run or one to face your corner?

The Gift of Being in a Corner. Each corner is an invitation to pause, self-assess, and realign. Use these moments to set PSMs that measure growth not in terms of external achievements but in resilience, patience and integrity. For example, your PSMs might focus on practicing mindfulness daily or journaling your emotions during challenging times. These small, consistent actions can help you track your progress and stay grounded even when circumstances are difficult.

Consider the corner you are in right now. It could be a demanding project, a strained relationship or a personal setback. Instead of focusing solely on escaping it, use this as an opportunity to coexist with discomfort and grow. Your PSMs could include small steps like reflecting on your thoughts daily, engaging in self-care routines or setting achievable short-term goals that bring clarity and strength over time.

Embracing the Lessons of the Corner. To truly harness the power of a corner, engage in regular self-reflection using the Thriveon Method's four questions:

- What did I achieve?
- What did I learn?
- What could I have done better?
- What must I change?

These questions are powerful tools for understanding what the corner is teaching you. Answering them provides clarity and illuminates a path forward; not always an immediate solution, but a deeper understanding of your growth and resilience.

As you document your reflections, patterns will emerge recurring fears, consistent challenges, or hidden strengths. Recognizing these patterns empowers you to take control of your growth journey, even when external circumstances remain uncertain.

The Courage to Stay. Staying in the corner rather than fleeing it requires immense courage. It means resisting the urge to take shortcuts, compromise your values, or blame others. Instead, it involves fully embracing the discomfort, knowing that every storm you weather builds the strength needed for the next challenge.

Think of sailors navigating a storm. They cannot control the wind, but they can adjust their sails, steady their course, and trust their skills to guide them through. Facing a corner is no different. By staying present, learning to navigate the chaos and holding steady, you grow into a person equipped to handle life's future tempests with confidence and grace.

From Good to Great – The Power of Resilience. True greatness does not come from easy victories but from the hard-earned wisdom gained through struggle. Each corner is a forge, shaping you into a more resilient, insightful version of yourself. The key is not merely to survive but to emerge transformed, stronger, wiser, and more aligned with your purpose.

Stay in your corner, face the discomfort and let it refine you. By embracing the lessons of the corner and setting measurable goals for resilience, you build a philosophy of structured, meaningful growth. Life can corner you, but it cannot confine you.

> Another corner, I painfully experienced. In 2017, I decided, to join a political party in Malta and contested as a candidate in the general election (with the benefit of hindsight, I now realize it was for the wrong reasons). The party, which had been in opposition since 2013, had a long history in government, holding power for 25 years prior to that. I was approved as a candidate in April 2017, under the impression that my first electoral contest would occur around May 2018, giving me roughly a year to prepare.

But, as life often does, it threw me a curveball. On 1 May 2017, the prime minister announced a snap election for June 2017. My preparation time was slashed from 12 months to six weeks and, to make matters worse, I was boarding a flight to the UK for a week-long sales training course. By the time I returned to Malta, I had just five weeks to run a campaign with no political experience and no understanding of how the party organization functioned.

I was completely lost.

Feeling the weight of this overwhelming corner, I made a difficult but necessary decision to be honest about my situation. I reached out to the party leader, explaining my predicament. While sympathetic, the leader's hands were tied due to the optics of favouritism during a campaign. However, he connected me with an experienced campaign manager, Simon Castillo. Simon and I clicked immediately. His guidance, experience, and sheer perseverance saw me through this whirlwind campaign. Simon, thank you.

Though I performed well, I did not win a seat in parliament, and I was content with that outcome. I assumed my political chapter had come to an end.

The Corner Tightens. Yet, fate had other plans. In March 2020, a sitting member of parliament resigned, triggering a bi-election in the district I had contested. Unexpectedly, I found myself sworn in as a member of Parliament. This new corner was even tighter than the first. Now, I was thrust further into the public eye, navigating the complexities of political life.

When I entered politics, I promised myself one thing: I would not let it change who I am. I like who I am, and I remain determined to protect that identity. However, the nature of politics slowly began to erode my happiness. I found myself surrounded by bad energy. Social gatherings, once a source of joy, became unbearable as conversations inevitably turned to politics.

The corner became suffocating. At times, I wanted to walk away entirely, to resign, to escape the toxicity, and to reclaim my peace. But I realized that leaving would create another corner. How would those who voted for me feel if I abandoned them? I had made a commitment, and I knew I had to honour it.

LESSONS LEARNED FROM THE CORNER

1. **Time Is a Healer:**
   I learned that some corners cannot be solved by brute force or immediate action. They require patience, perspective, and the willingness to let time run its course.

2. **Embrace the Challenge:**
   Walking away might provide temporary relief, but it risks creating a new set of challenges. Sometimes, the best course is to embrace the discomfort and give your best within the constraints of the situation.

3. **Own Your Decisions:**
   This corner was one of my own making, and I had to take responsibility for it. Accepting that this was a result of my choices helped me find clarity and focus on doing my best rather than succumbing to regret.

4. **Separate Self-Worth from External Outcomes:**
   Just because I excelled in business did not mean I would thrive in politics. This experience taught me that failure in one area does not diminish my overall value or identity.

5. **Evaluate the Cost of Sacrifice:**
   The emotional toll of staying in this corner was significant, but so was the potential cost of leaving. I learned to weigh both sides thoughtfully, focusing on fulfilling my obligations while preserving my wellbeing.

6. **Exit Gracefully:**
   Not every project is meant to succeed. Sometimes, the most honourable path is to finish what you started, learn from the experience, and move on with grace and dignity.

This corner, though painful and challenging, became a profound teacher. It reminded me that growth often comes not from easy victories but from enduring the hardest of struggles. While politics was not my calling, it reinforced my belief in perseverance and the importance of staying true to myself. As I prepare to leave this corner, I do so with a renewed commitment to never stop learning, even from the tightest spaces.

From Corner to Growth. When we stop viewing corners as traps and start seeing them as transformative spaces, something profound happens. The corner no longer feels restrictive; it becomes a launchpad, a moment of reflection and clarity that prepares us for new possibilities. For those who hold steady, who face their corners with integrity, patience, and self-compassion, the rewards are immeasurable.

Corners are not where we lose ourselves; they are where we find the parts of us that are brave enough to stay, learn, and grow. Every human being is like a jigsaw puzzle, pieced together by their experiences. Corners are opportunities to discover and assemble the pieces, shaping you into a stronger, more resilient version of yourself.

As you reflect on your own corners, remember this: each one faced with honesty, each challenge endured with grace, is a step closer to unlocking your greatest potential. This is how you grow from good to great.

But there is one more thing to consider: the role of your inner dialogue. Often, the greatest challenge in any corner is not the external pressure but the inner enemy that whispers doubt, fear, and defeat. The voice inside can either push you to rise or pull you deeper into despair.

Do not let your worst enemy, the one within, get the better of you. In the next chapter, we will confront this internal adversary and learn how to transform it from a force of self-sabotage into a source of strength. Let's move forward.

SOMETHING TO PONDER

The moment when you **MOST** feel like giving up is the **INSTANT** when you must find it in you to press ahead.

Call to Action: This is a good time to reflect and take note of your thoughts.

1. **Spot Your Corner**: Ask yourself, "What is holding me back? Peer pressure, social media, or fear of failure?" Write it down to make it clear.

2. **Weigh the Cost**: Challenge yourself: "What do I lose if I stay here? What could I gain if I step out one small step at a time?"

3. **Plan Your Win**: Pick one action to break free. Whether it is speaking up, trying something new, or limiting social media time. Celebrate the growth it brings!

TAKE THE NEXT STEP IN YOUR JOURNEY

To truly embrace **The Power of Corners**, you must shift your mindset from seeing challenges as setbacks to recognizing them as **opportunities for growth**. The next step is to analyse, reframe, and develop an action plan to navigate through your toughest moments with confidence.

This exercise is not just about overcoming challenges, it is about **building resilience, self-awareness, and a forward-thinking mindset**. The clarity you gain will empower you to turn discomfort into personal development, ultimately guiding you toward a stronger, more confident version of yourself.

Before moving on to the next chapter, commit to **embracing your corners**. Your growth is waiting on the other side.

TURNING TOWARD THE LIGHT: REFLECTIONS FOR GROWTH

Reflection 1 – **The Shadow of Freedom**

Many of us live in invisible prisons, confined not by physical bars but by the weight of self-doubt, limiting beliefs, and perceived judgments from others. These walls are not real, but they feel solid. We stand behind the bars, convinced we are stuck, unable to see a way out.

But what if you turned your perspective? Behind you, a light of hope shines, always present, even if unnoticed. This light casts a shadow beyond the bars, a shadow that represents freedom. It shows you that your potential, your best self, exists just outside this self-imposed cell.

Freedom is within reach, but it requires turning toward the light. It demands courage, commitment to self-growth, and a belief that you are capable of more. The shadow of freedom is not a mirage; it is a glimpse of what is possible when you trust yourself and take the first step.

Reflection: What bars are holding you back? Can you turn towards the light, toward your hope?

Call to Action: Stop, take a few minutes, and reflect upon the following:

- Identify one limiting belief that feels like a 'bar' in your life.
- Reflect on what the light of hope looks like for you. Is it a goal, a dream, or a personal value?
- What is the one action you can take today to move closer to the shadow of freedom?

9

YOUR WORST ENEMY

The Inner Critic in a Modern World. In the chapter Corners, we explored the challenges that life throws at us, the external obstacles, and circumstances that force us to grow. But, often, the hardest battles are not fought in the outside world. They are fought within.

Your worst enemy is not always an external force; it is the voice in your head that whispers, *"You are not good enough."* This inner critic thrives in the tight spaces of corners, magnifying self-doubt and turning moments of challenge into spirals of negativity.

This internal voice, the inner critic, can be relentless, amplifying every misstep and overshadowing even the greatest achievements. It keeps you trapped in cycles of self-sabotage, paralyzed by fear, and disconnected from your potential. And in today's modern world of constant comparison and societal pressure, this voice has only grown louder. A missed opportunity, a single mistake, or even an offhand comment from someone else can feed this enemy, making it stronger and harder to ignore.

But here is the truth: this voice is not your reality. It is a distortion, a liar disguised as your conscience. To overcome it, you must first recognize its influence. The corners you face in life may test your resilience, but your inner dialogue determines whether you rise or retreat.

Critical and objective thinking is your greatest weapon against the inner critic. When emotions and subjectivity cloud your perspective, it becomes easy to lose clarity and veer off course. This is why cultivating self-awareness is essential. Whether you are reflecting on Personal Success Metrics (PSMs), the signposts that guide and measure your growth, or making decisions in your personal or professional life, emotional bias and self-doubt can distort your judgment and undermine your progress.

Your mind can either be your greatest ally or your worst enemy. It is imperative to develop the discipline to separate facts from feelings and align your thoughts with truth and objectivity. When you master this, you reclaim control, quiet the critic, and strengthen your resilience. The journey to overcoming the inner voice begins here, by challenging its lies and replacing them with empowering truths. Let's explore how to take this next step.

> From my experience, working with young people at university and in business, I have come to realize how social media can in fact feed our worst enemy.
>
> Imagine standing in front of a distorted mirror at a funhouse, one that stretches and skews your reflection. This is what social media often does to your self-perception. It reflects an idealized world where everyone seems more successful, more attractive, and happier than you. But like the funhouse mirror, this version of reality is warped.

Scrolling through endless highlight reels, you may find yourself questioning your worth:

- "Why is my life not as exciting as theirs?"
- "Why am I not achieving as much as they are?"
- "Why do I not look like that?"

These thoughts trigger your inner critic, making you feel like you are falling short. Social media is not the enemy itself, but it acts as a catalyst, amplifying your insecurities and feeding the voice that says you are not enough.

Practical Reflection. Take a moment to review your social media habits. Are there accounts that make you feel small or inadequate? Unfollow them. Curate your digital space to reflect positivity, authenticity and inspiration. Treat it as an extension of your mind; only allow in what uplifts you.

Validation Dependency. The Like Trap, one of the cruel tricks of your inner critic, is convincing you that your worth depends on external validation. How many likes, comments, or followers you have has become a measure of your value. But the truth is, no amount of digital approval will ever silence your inner critic or express your true value. Think of the last time you posted something online. Did you find yourself checking your phone repeatedly to see how people responded?

This behaviour traps you in a cycle of seeking external reassurance, leaving your self-worth vulnerable to the fleeting opinions of others. In a practical way, you must pursue a Digital Detox Challenge. For one day, avoid checking your social media accounts. Use this time to journal about your strengths, passions, and accomplishments. Notice how stepping away from the digital noise helps you reconnect with your inner voice, the one that truly matters.

The Mental Health Connection. Your inner critic does not just live in your mind; it affects your mental health in profound ways. Constant self-criticism can lead to anxiety, depression, and chronic stress. You might find yourself stuck in thought patterns that leave you drained, defeated, and unable to move forward.

Recognizing these patterns is the first step. Does your inner voice often say things like:

- “I will never be good at this.”
- “Why even try? I am just going to fail.”
- “I do not deserve success.”
- “Everyone will think I am a fraud.”
- “I am not as smart/talented as others, so why bother?”
- “If I make a mistake, it will prove I am a failure.”
- “Success is for people who already have everything figured out, not me.”

- "One wrong move and I will lose everything I have worked for."
- "I have to be perfect; anything less means I am not good enough."

These are distortions, not facts. They are lies that your inner critic uses to hold you back. Take some time, write down these negative thoughts as they arise, then challenge them. For example, if you think, "I am not good enough," ask yourself, "What evidence do I have for this?" Replace the distortion with a constructive truth, such as, "I am learning, and every step forward counts."

Practical steps to conquer your inner critic consist of:

Mindfulness Matters. Ground yourself in the present. When your inner critic grows loud, pause and breathe deeply. A simple technique like inhaling for four seconds, holding for four seconds, and exhaling for four seconds can reduce anxiety and help you regain control.

Celebrate Small Wins. Your inner critic thrives on perfectionism, but life is not about grand achievements alone. Start celebrating your small wins, finishing a task, learning something new, or even getting out of bed on a tough day.

> **Create a "Wins Journal."** At the end of each day, jot down three things you accomplished, no matter how small. Over time, this habit shifts your focus from what you lack to what you have achieved.
>
> **Ask for Help**. It is not weakness to seek support. Whether it is a therapist, coach, or trusted friend, talking about your struggles helps you gain perspective and find solutions.
>
> It is only you that can redefine your mirror. The mirror you face every day is not just the one hanging on your wall. It is the reflection you carry in your mind. While social media, stress and self-doubt distort this reflection, you have the power to adjust the lens. The next time you hear your inner critic whisper, challenge it. Remember, the strongest weapon you have against your worst enemy is the voice of self-compassion and belief. Your best self is not waiting for likes or approval; it is waiting for you to recognize it in the mirror and take that first step forward.

Your inner voice, your worst enemy, or your greatest supporter, is the foundation of your growth or the source of your stagnation. It feeds on both facts and perceptions, shaping your beliefs about what you can or cannot do. Left unchecked, this inner critic works hand-in-hand with another invisible barrier: your comfort zone. While the inner critic whispers doubt and magnifies fear, the comfort zone creates the illusion of safety, keeping you anchored in routines that hinder growth. Together, they form a powerful duo that limits your potential, reinforcing internal barriers and external challenges.

Objectively and critically think about the comfort zone. Your comfort zone is a space that feels predictable and safe, a place where decisions carry minimal risk, and routines remain unchallenged. While this zone offers a sense of control, it is a deceptive sanctuary. It lures you into a state of inertia, where the ease of familiarity masks the cost of stagnation. Remaining in the comfort zone minimizes stress in the moment but deprives you of the challenges necessary for growth and self-discovery.

The Comfort Zone and the Fear Zone. Psychologically, the comfort zone provides a sense of relief by reducing perceived risk. Yet, it is often built on the foundation of a deeper and more restrictive space: the fear zone. The fear zone is populated by the perceptions of failure, embarrassment, loss, or change, barriers that appear real but are often self-constructed by the inner critic. These fears are natural, as humans are wired to prioritize safety and avoid uncertainty. However, unchecked fear anchors us to routines, convincing us that stepping out is unnecessary or too risky.

How Internal Barriers and External Challenges Work Together. The inner critic feeds on both external challenges and internal barriers. External challenges are facts, the obstacles or difficulties you must confront in the real world. Internal barriers, on the other hand, are perceptions, the fears, doubts, and narratives created by your inner critic. For example:

- **Challenge (fact)**: You lack a specific skill for a project.
- **Barrier (perception)**: "I will never be good enough, so why even try?"

Breaking free from the comfort zone requires acknowledging these fears without letting them control your actions. It is not about eliminating fear but learning to work through it by cultivating resilience and building confidence step-by-step.

The Cost of Staying Comfortable. Staying within the comfort zone may feel secure, but it dulls your potential. The brain thrives on challenges and when you engage with new experiences, it releases dopamine, the neurotransmitter associated with growth and learning. Over time, this process creates new neural pathways, helping you expand your identity and capabilities. Staying comfortable, on the other hand, minimizes stimulation and limits the brain's natural drive for exploration, leaving you feeling stuck and uninspired.

Breaking Free: Small Steps to Build Resilience. To move beyond the comfort zone, you do not need to take a giant leap; instead, start with small, consistent actions. Here are some recommended strategies to assist you to break free.

Acknowledge the Facts and Perceptions:

- Identify the external challenges (facts) that you are facing.
- Separate these from internal barriers (perceptions) like self-doubt or fear of failure.

Challenge Your Inner Critic:

- When you hear self-defeating thoughts, write them down. Ask yourself, "Is this true, or is this my fear speaking?" Replace distortions with constructive truths.

Set Incremental Goals:

- Take small steps out of your comfort zone. For example, if you fear public speaking, start by sharing your ideas in small meetings. Gradually increase the challenge to build confidence.

Build a Daily Reflection Habit:

- Use the Thriveon Method's four questions:
    - What did I achieve?
    - What did I learn?
    - What could I have done better?
    - What must I change?

This process allows you to track progress, celebrate small wins, and address fears head-on.

Redefine Success:

- Success is not perfection; it is progress. Celebrate the effort you put into stepping out of your comfort zone, even if the results are not immediate.

The Mirror Never Lies. When you stay within your comfort zone, the mirror reflects stagnation, but when you face your fears and act, the mirror begins to reflect growth, resilience, and possibility. The inner critic and the comfort zone are powerful adversaries, but they are not undefeatable. By practicing self-awareness, challenging your perceptions, and stepping into discomfort, you transform both obstacles into opportunities for growth.

As you continue this journey, remember: your comfort zone may feel safe, but growth lies just beyond its borders.

From my experience, it is easy to tell ourselves we are invincible when we are in the rhythm of a disciplined routine. Since I was 35 years old, despite a demanding schedule and a fast-paced lifestyle, I was loyal to my personal well being and health PSM. I made exercise a non-negotiable priority, hitting the gym four to five times a week, running outdoors, tracking my performance, and consistently setting higher goals. When traveling, whether for business or leisure, I never left home without my running shoes, and my commitment to staying out of my comfort zone was unwavering.

But then, as it did for so many, COVID-19 changed everything. The pandemic reshaped our lives overnight. Gyms closed, restrictions limited outdoor activities, and I found myself staring at the gym equipment I had at home, a setup that seemed weak and substandard compared to my usual environment. But in truth, none of these factors – the closed gyms, the outdoor limits, the quality of my equipment, were the real obstacles. They were excuses.

During the pandemic, I found myself in an uncharacteristic state of inertia. With the familiar rhythms of work and life suddenly disrupted, I initially struggled to adapt. For weeks, I found solace in distractions like television and social media, convincing myself that waiting for normal to return was the best course of action. But the more I waited, the more I realized that normal was gone and it was not coming back anytime soon.

In what felt like no time at all, I slipped into a free fall that landed me squarely in the comfort zone. There I was, at home in comfortable clothes, spending my days online, and gradually watching my once unbreakable commitment to my health fade away. The sense of achievement I used to feel at the gym vanished, replaced by a kind of apathy I had never known. And I convinced myself, as so many did, that the pandemic was a reason to simply enjoy life, skip the pain of exercise, and take things easy.

But soon enough, the signs of this shift began to show. I gained weight, I started feeling more tired, and, without realizing it, I began losing confidence. I no longer recognized the person I saw in the mirror, a reflection that, as I have always said, never lies. My physical wellness had always been a pillar of my personal and professional life, a constant amid any chaos. But here I was, held captive by the comfort zone, trapped in a cycle that became one of the hardest to break.

I remember one day, standing in my kitchen, overwhelmed by the silence of an empty house. That was my turning point. I decided that, instead of waiting, I would reclaim my agency. I set small, actionable goals, starting with just 15 minutes a day to journal my thoughts and outline new aspirations. It was not easy, but each small step brought a sense of purpose back into my days.

What shocked me most was how difficult it was to climb back out. Every excuse felt justified; after all, had not we been through so much? Age became a convenient excuse, too, whispering that perhaps I did not have to push myself as I had before. It took me several months to overcome this slump. I learned, painfully, that comfort zones do not just keep us stagnant; they steal our vitality and dampen our spirits.

Looking back, it was this climb, slow and grueling, that ultimately brought me here, to the keyboard, writing this book. I realized that the fight to leave the comfort zone is not just about physical fitness or PSMs; it is about reclaiming the person you know you can be. Comfort, I now understand, can become a prison that limits who we are and what we are capable of. And this book is my way of sharing the tools, the insights, and the stories that helped me rise again. I know what it feels like to be stuck, and I know how powerful it feels to break free.

Throughout this time, I reflected, and I took away a few lessons that I am sharing with you. This experience taught me a profound lesson: even in times of chaos, we have the power to create order. I learned that discomfort, though unwelcome, is often the catalyst for growth. And in the midst of uncertainty, the act of simply moving forward, no matter how small the step, can transform fear into opportunity.

Overall, I learned that taking things and people for granted can lead to complacency, fostering comfort zones that may result in personal disarray and the erosion of meaningful relationships.

1. **Taking Things for Granted**
   When we become accustomed to certain conveniences or resources, we may overlook their value. This complacency can lead to neglecting maintenance or failing to express gratitude, resulting in potential loss or deterioration of these assets.

2. **Taking People for Granted**
   In relationships, assuming that others will always be there without acknowledging their efforts can cause feelings of unappreciation. This neglect may lead to emotional distance, resentment, and eventually the breakdown of the relationship. For instance, consistently failing to recognize a partner's contributions can erode the foundation of mutual respect and affection.

3. **Comfort Zones and Their Consequences**
   Both scenarios contribute to the formation of comfort zones, states of complacency where growth is stunted. Remaining in these zones can lead to personal stagnation and the deterioration of relationships. By not challenging ourselves or nurturing our connections, we risk losing valuable aspects of our lives.

4. **Preventing Negative Outcomes**
   To avoid these pitfalls, it is essential to practice mindfulness and gratitude. Regularly acknowledging the value of both things and people in our lives encourages proactive care and appreciation. This approach not only preserves our assets but also strengthens our relationships, fostering a more fulfilling and connected life.

Resistance to change is one of the most subtle yet powerful adversaries on your journey to self-growth. It often disguises itself as rational excuses: *"This is not the right time," "What if I fail?"* or *"I am already doing enough."* These thoughts are rooted in a fear of the unknown and a natural inclination to cling to what feels safe, even if it no longer serves you. Recognizing this resistance is essential because it exposes the internal battle between your desire for growth and the comfort of the status quo.

To overcome this enemy, start small. Commit to one meaningful action each day that challenges your current habits or beliefs. Each small victory chips away at the wall of resistance, showing you that change is not only possible, but also empowering. The enemy within thrives on inaction and self-doubt, but it cannot survive the momentum of intentional effort.

Resistance to change does not always show itself in dramatic ways. Often, it hides in plain sight, embedded in the routines we follow and the small decisions we make every day. From my experience, I am, in many ways, a creature of habit. I find myself sticking to familiar routes even if there is traffic, dining at the same restaurants and choosing the same fuel station, even when it is out of my way. I justify this behaviour by calling myself a loyalist. But am I truly loyal or am I simply too comfortable with what I know? Too accustomed to familiar faces, menus and paths to consider the possibility of something better? Am I avoiding new choices because I am a loyalist or am I resisting change because it feels easier not to think about it?

These types of habits I shared above influenced my behaviour outside work. While in my professional life I lived outside the comfort zone and always thrived going from good to great, I often felt that I owed it to myself to stay within my comfort zone in my personal life. Over time, I came to realize that this behaviour negatively influenced my sense of adventure and my readiness to explore new things and places, especially during holidays with my family. It is thanks to my wife that I managed to break this downward spiral behaviour that was robbing me of so many wonderful experiences. I finally came to understand that

> I must thrive to grow in every aspect of this beautiful life. The rich experiences I gained by breaking this pattern made me realize that growth is not just for professional life, it is a gift we must embrace in every corner of our existence.

The Path from Comfort to Growth. Beyond the fear zone lies the learning zone, a space where discovery, growth, and transformation begin. This is where individuals step beyond the confines of their comfort zones, not only acquiring new skills but also gaining valuable insights about themselves. Psychologists call this self-directed learning, a process of redefining personal narratives and expanding self-awareness.

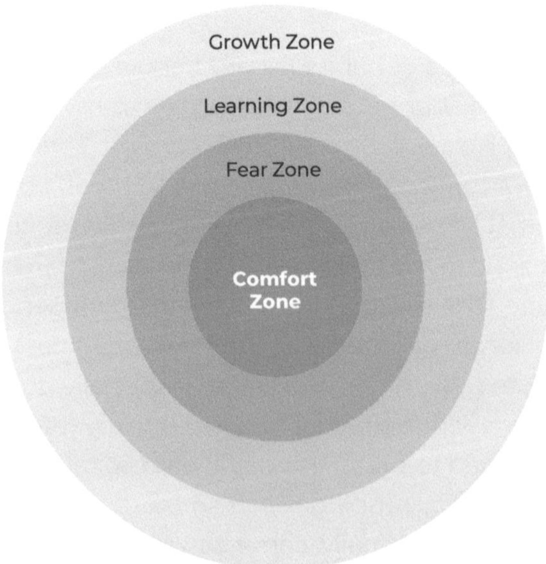

In the learning zone, individuals set new goals, celebrate achievements, and deepen their self-knowledge. This process requires consistent, structured self-reflection, a practice that helps shift mental limits and fosters adaptability. Instead of waiting for external circumstances to change, individuals learn to adjust their inner mindset, developing confidence in their ability to face challenges and reducing their reliance on external validation.

Strategies to Overcome Emotional Subjectivity. Overcoming the influence of emotional subjectivity and resistance to change requires intentional practice. Here are strategies to help you remain objective and aligned with your growth:

1. **Practice Self-Awareness**
   - Recognize emotional triggers and reflect on moments when emotions distort your perception.
   - Pause and ask, *"Am I reacting emotionally, or responding based on facts?"*

2. **Separate Facts from Feelings**
   - Write down the facts of a situation separately from how you feel about it.
   - This practice helps distinguish reality from emotional bias.

3. **Ask Thought-Provoking Questions**
   - Challenge your thoughts with questions like:
     - *"What evidence supports this thought?"*
     - *"What would I advise someone else in my situation?"*

4. **Engage in Structured Reflection**
    - Use the Thriveon Method's four questions to track growth and maintain objectivity:
        - *Today, what did I achieve?*
        - *Today, what did I learn?*
        - *Today, what could I have done better?*
        - *What must I change?*

5. **Seek Diverse Perspectives**
    - Share your challenges with trusted individuals to gain fresh, unbiased viewpoints.

6. **Develop Emotional Regulation Skills**
    - Use techniques such as deep breathing, progressive muscle relaxation, or mindfulness to calm emotional reactions and create space for rational thinking.

7. **Set Clear Goals and Boundaries**
    - Define clear, measurable goals and boundaries to avoid overthinking or letting emotions dominate your decisions.

8. **Practice Detachment**
    - Ask yourself: *"Will this matter a year from now?"* This mindset prioritizes long-term impact over short-term emotions.

9. **Celebrate Progress, Not Perfection**
    - Focus on small victories and incremental growth, reinforcing the belief that progress is more important than perfection.

10. **Reflect on Past Lessons**
    - Look back on moments where emotions clouded judgment. Use these experiences to refine your decision-making skills.

From Learning to Growth. As you embrace the learning zone, you gradually transition into the growth zone. This is where you pursue higher goals, embrace challenges, and begin to embody the best version of yourself. In this zone, you gain clarity about your strengths, continuously set new aspirations, and move closer to self-actualization.

However, growth is not a destination, it is an ongoing cycle. Over time, the growth zone becomes your new comfort zone, signalling that it is time to seek fresh challenges. This dynamic process of expanding your comfort zone ensures continuous development and prevents stagnation.

The Hidden Cost of Staying Comfortable. While the comfort zone feels safe, it comes with hidden costs. Avoiding challenges may shield you from short-term stress but deprives you of long-term growth. Studies show that individuals who remain in their comfort zones often experience lower satisfaction, fewer opportunities for self-improvement, and a higher risk of burnout due to monotony.

Staying too comfortable fosters a fixed mindset, reducing mental resilience, and limiting personal potential.

Structured Self-Reflection: A Tool for Growth. The key to escaping the comfort zone lies in structured self-reflection. Through consistent evaluation of your actions, goals, and challenges, you develop the habit of holding yourself accountable. The Thriveon Method encourages you to see setbacks not as failures but as stepping-stones toward success.

By engaging in daily reflection, you become better equipped to navigate the cycle of comfort, fear, learning, and growth. This process builds resilience, helping you identify areas where you are stagnating and inspiring you to pursue meaningful growth.

Embracing the Growth Cycle. Growth requires revisiting and redefining your comfort zones. Over time, as you expand your horizons, the challenges you once faced with trepidation become opportunities for self-discovery. The cycle of moving from comfort to growth is not linear; it is an evolving process that continues throughout life.

Comfort zones are not inherently negative, but they become dangerous when they limit your potential. Choosing to step beyond comfort means embracing the discomfort of growth and uncovering new possibilities. The journey from the comfort zone to the growth zone is challenging, but it leads to a life of greater resilience, fulfillment, and purpose.

From Enemy to Ally: The Next Step in Your Journey. Your inner critic, the fear of change, and the allure of comfort are all challenges you can overcome. Each step forward teaches you to face your worst enemy with courage, persistence, and clarity. As you master these internal battles, you prepare for the next stage: charting your path.

In the next chapter, Your Journey, we will explore how to align your purpose, goals, and Personal Success Metrics (PSMs) to create a road map for meaningful growth. This is your moment to take control, to move with intention, and thrive.

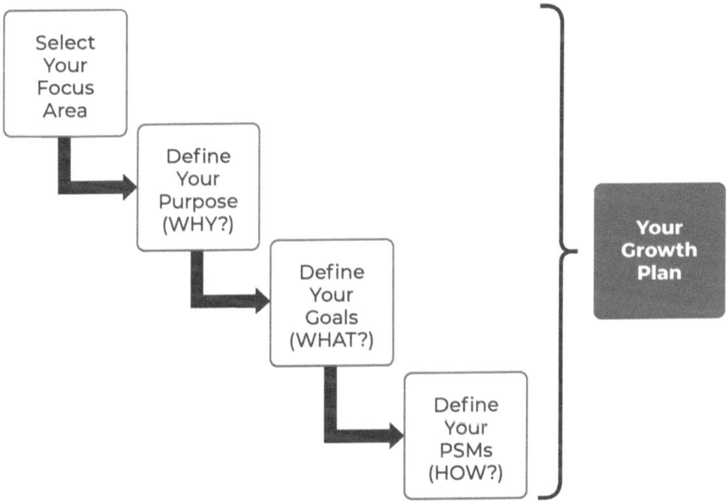

SOMETHING TO PONDER

PAIN is the doorway into the **DEEP**.
It burns away fakeness, fear, and arrogance
that belongs to the **EGO**.

Call to Action: This is a good time to reflect and take note of your thoughts.

1. **Quiet Your Inner Critic**: Write down one negative thought you have had about yourself today. Now, challenge it by writing one positive truth that counters it.

2. **Stop the Comparison**: Pick one social media account that makes you feel less than or stuck. Unfollow or mute it today. It is time to focus on your growth, not theirs.

3. **Take One Brave Step**: What is one small action you have avoided because of self-doubt? Do it now, whether it is speaking up, starting a project, or asking for help.

TAKE THE NEXT STEP IN YOUR JOURNEY

To truly overcome **your worst enemy**, you must break free from the invisible barriers of **comfort and fear** that are holding you back. The next step is to **identify where you are stuck, recognize how it limits your potential, and take bold action to push past it**.

This exercise is not just about identifying where you are stuck, it is about **challenging yourself to take action, embrace discomfort, and build the confidence to grow beyond limitations**. The clarity you gain will help you shift from playing it safe to taking control of your growth and potential.

Before moving on to the next chapter, commit to stepping beyond your comfort zone. **Your greatest growth lies just outside of it**.

TURNING TOWARD THE LIGHT: REFLECTIONS FOR GROWTH

Reflection 2 – **The Comfort Zone Trap**

The comfort zone is a space of safety, predictability, and routine. It feels warm and familiar, a place where risk is minimized, and discomfort is avoided. But this sense of security can also be deceptive. Over time, the comfort zone becomes a trap, a silent thief of growth, stealing opportunities, potential, and the chance to become more than you are today.

Imagine being inside a cozy room with soft lighting and a locked door. The room feels safe but, as time passes, you notice the walls are closing in, shrinking the space you inhabit. Fear of stepping out keeps you locked in, even as the walls stifle your creativity, ambition, and dreams.

Life outside the comfort zone can feel uncertain and daunting, but it is where transformation happens. Growth does not come from repeating what you have always done; it comes from venturing into the unknown, taking risks, and embracing the possibility of failure as a stepping-stone to success.

Reflection: Where have you grown too comfortable? What opportunities await you just outside your walls? The comfort zone may feel like safety, but freedom and fulfilment lie beyond it.

Call to Action: Stop, take a few minutes, and reflect upon the following:

- **Identify Your Trap**: Ask yourself, what areas of my life feel safe but stagnant? Write down one thing you are avoiding because it feels uncomfortable or risky.
- **Imagine the Possibilities**: Visualize what is on the other side of your comfort zone. What could change if you embraced the unknown? Write one opportunity that excites you.
- **Take the First Step**: Commit to a small action today that pushes your boundaries: a conversation, a new experience, or a challenge. Growth starts with one step beyond what feels safe.

10

YOUR JOURNEY

Agility is a word that echoes across boardrooms, gyms, and motivational talks. It is a concept that many speak of, but few truly understand. Agility is not just about speed or flexibility; it is about adaptability, resilience, and purpose-driven action. In the context of personal growth, agility is more than a buzzword; it is a mindset.

In the previous chapter, we confronted our worst enemy: the inner voice that feeds self-doubt and thrives on comfort. We explored the cycle of moving from the comfort zone to the growth zone, embracing self-reflection and resilience to rise beyond fear and inertia. Now, the question is, how do you sustain this growth? How do you translate these insights into purposeful action? The answer lies in developing mental agility, the cornerstone of personal transformation.

Mental agility is about being adaptable, resilient, and forward-thinking. It equips you to navigate the challenges of life with grace, turning obstacles into opportunities for growth. It is not about conforming to the circumstance's life has dealt you; it is about mastering what you can change and finding strength in what you cannot.

Each of us carries a unique set of unchangeable characteristics like our height, age, cultural background, and inherent traits. These factors shape who we are but should never limit us. The danger lies in allowing these fixed elements to dictate our self-image, convincing us that growth is out of reach. Transformation is not about wishing away what cannot be changed; it is about cultivating the areas of your life that you can influence.

Your critical success factors being your attitude, skills, work ethic, emotional intelligence, and ability to set and achieve goals are fully within your control. These are the keys to unlocking the agile mindset that propels you forward on your journey. Agility is not something you are born with; it is a skill you develop through intentional effort.

Your journey begins the moment you decide to take ownership of your growth. True change does not happen through dramatic overnight transformations. It is built through daily habits, small incremental steps and intentional choices that align your efforts with your aspirations.

You are not defined by what you cannot change, but by how you rise to challenges. Agility means taking charge of your story, stepping outside of passivity, and embracing your potential for growth. Each step you take strengthens your ability to meet life's challenges and aligns you more closely with the best version of yourself.

In this dynamic and fast-paced world, personal growth, and career development, one truth stands out: you are in control of your progress. When you approach your personal and professional development with intentionality, structure, and discipline, you do not merely survive life's challenges, you thrive through them.

This chapter is your call to take charge of your journey. It is an invitation to embrace the Thriveon Method's structured self-reflection, using it not just as a tool for self-improvement but as a guide for intentional growth.

Consider how often individuals wait passively for feedback, whether in performance reviews, professional evaluations, or even personal relationships. Too often, they allow others to define their worth. But imagine the power of reversing this dynamic. Picture yourself walking into any review, be it personal or professional, not as a passive recipient but as a confident participant, equipped with your own insights and reflections. This is the agility of the mind in action: owning your growth, measuring your progress, and leading the conversation about your contributions and value.

Your journey begins now, and it is yours to design, one intentional step at a time.

The Power of Preparation and Ownership: Preparation is the cornerstone of success in any meaningful discussion or review process. Early in my career as CEO of 6PM, a company whose success heavily depended on recurring annuity revenue, I learned this lesson the hard way. Our business model revolved around renewable annual agreements with our customers, and my role was to ensure these relationships thrived, so contracts were renewed year after year.

I adopted a clear strategy: meet with each customer twice during their contract period, once at the midpoint (six months in) and again one month before the renewal. These meetings were not just check-ins; they were performance reviews of our business relationship. Much like the 180° and 360° performance reviews that employees experience in their careers, these meetings had one objective: to prove value.

Walking into these meetings unprepared was not an option. It was not enough to show up and passively listen to their thoughts about our service, products, or costs. While listening is critical, I knew I had to do more. I had to walk in equipped with hard data, actionable insights, and a clear narrative that demonstrated the value 6PM delivered.

Here is what preparation looked like for me: I analysed how many incidents each customer reported, the average time it took us to resolve those incidents, and the total hours our team dedicated to supporting them. I converted this raw data into visual presentations such as graphs, tables, and reports, making it impossible for anyone to overlook the value we brought to their organization. With these tools, I did not just participate in the meetings; I led them. My preparation gave me the confidence to show my customers that 6PM was not just a vendor, we were a valuable business partner invested in their success enabling them to realize tangible business value.

This is the same mindset you must bring to your performance review meetings with your boss, lectures, personal coaches, or team members. Treat these meetings not as passive evaluations where you sit and receive feedback but as opportunities to take charge of your narrative. Like my customer meetings, your performance review is your moment to demonstrate that you are in control of your goals, you embrace your PSMs, and you measure and manage your own growth.

By preparing thoroughly, you equip yourself to present not only what you have achieved but also what you have learned, where you can improve, and how you plan to evolve. This preparation is not just about impressing your reviewer; it is about building your own confidence and self-awareness. When you have the data and insights to back up your contributions, you establish yourself as an indispensable part of the organization, someone who continually delivers value and belongs at the table.

Much like my role at 6PM, where I reviewed customer-related data daily, weekly or bi-weekly to prepare for crucial meetings, you should commit to the Thriveon self-reflection process. Use it to build visibility into your own performance, what you have achieved, what you have learned, what pitfalls you have encountered, and what changes you made or need to make. This process is your key to growth, productivity, and excellence.

The attitude you bring to this process will shape your future. With consistent effort and discipline, you will not only rise to new heights but also inspire respect, secure promotions, and cement your sense of belonging within your organization. Your journey from good to great starts with taking ownership of your growth. This is the mindset and process that will unlock your true potential.

Why Structured Self-Reflection Matters. Think of your personal growth journey as mastering your craft. Each day is an opportunity to refine your skills, extract lessons from experiences, and take intentional steps forward. The Thriveon Method's structured self-reflection provides a clear framework to evaluate:

1. **What You Achieved**. Celebrate the wins, big or small, to reinforce positive behaviour.

2. **What You Learned**. Extract lessons from successes and setbacks alike. Growth is a continuous education.

3. **What You Could Have Done Better**. Examine pitfalls without judgment to identify opportunities for improvement.

4. **What You Must Change**. Take proactive steps to adapt, refine, and elevate your performance.

When practiced consistently, this process becomes more than a discipline; it evolves into a positive habit, a lifestyle that prioritizes progress and self-awareness.

Entering Performance Reviews with Confidence: The power of structured self-reflection shines brightest in performance reviews. Traditionally, these meetings are viewed as one-sided evaluations where individuals passively receive feedback. But imagine walking into your next review as an active participant, someone who takes charge of the discussion.

Using your structured self-reflection as a foundation, you can confidently articulate:

- **Your Achievements**: Showcase measurable outcomes and the impact of your contributions.
- **Lessons Learned**: Share how you have adapted to challenges and grown in your role.
- **Improvements Identified**: Demonstrate your commitment to progress by discussing areas you have actively worked on.
- **Plans for the Future**: Present clear strategies for continued growth and enhanced contributions

This approach establishes you as someone in control of their journey, a proactive, self-driven contributor.

Preparation: The Key to Success. Preparation is the secret ingredient for owning any performance review. Reflecting on my time as CEO of 6PM, I can draw parallels between my responsibility to secure customer contract renewals and preparing for personal performance reviews.

At 6PM, customer meetings were like performance reviews in the corporate world. I never walked into those meetings unprepared. Instead, I relied on:

- **Data Analysis**: Tracking incidents resolved, average response times, and hours invested in the client's success.
- **Visual Presentations**: Using graphs, tables, and reports to make my points clear and undeniable.
- **Value Proposition**: Demonstrating how our partnership delivered tangible results and benefits.

These efforts transformed our meetings from routine discussions into collaborative opportunities for growth. By highlighting both achievements and areas for improvement, we built stronger relationships, and positioned ourselves as indispensable partners.

Now, imagine applying this approach to your own growth journey. Just as I measured 6PM's value, you can measure and present your own.

Why This Process Works for You and Others. Structured self-reflection benefits not only your reviewers but also yourself.

1. **For Your Reviewer:**
    - Demonstrating accountability and growth sets you apart as proactive and results-oriented.

- Sharing measurable outcomes highlights your commitment to delivering value.
- Presenting improvement areas shows maturity and a growth mindset.

2. **For Yourself:**
    - Measuring your achievements builds confidence and reinforces self-trust.
    - Aligning your actions with personal goals enforces your purpose.
    - Developing insights into your own progress shifts the need for external validation to internal satisfaction.

The true transformation happens when you wake up feeling proud, not because of external recognition, but because you know you are moving closer to the person you aspire to become.

How does this happen?

1. **Intentional Actions**. Align your Personal Success Metrics (PSMs) with what matters to you. Whether it is reading a book, improving a skill, or achieving work-life balance, these small actions compound over time.

2. **Celebrating Wins**. Turning simple victories, such as drinking more water or meeting a fitness goal, into fuel for sustained momentum.

3. **Building Self-Trust**. Each time you follow through on a commitment, you reinforce the belief that you can rely on yourself.

The Power of Incremental Growth. The journey from good to great is not a result of sporadic effort; it is the culmination of small, consistent actions. Taking just 20 to 30 minutes each day to reflect on your PSMs, track progress, and plan your next steps is a transformative investment in yourself.

When you dedicate yourself to this process, you:

1. **Gain Clarity**: Understand where you stand and what needs to be done.

2. **Build Momentum**: Small, intentional actions lead to exponential growth over time.

3. **Boost Confidence**: Through self-reflection, you become more self-aware and prepared for challenges.

Your Growth Journey Awaits. Just as I prepared relentlessly to secure renewals and growth at 6PM, you, too, can prepare for your own success. With structured self-reflection, every day is an opportunity to take charge of your journey. Armed with insights, clarity, and purpose, you can confidently lead the conversation in your performance reviews, team discussions, or personal evaluations.

Growth is not about one monumental change; it is about committing to small, daily improvements. It is about embracing the Thriveon Method, celebrating progress, and recognizing that the journey from good to great is yours to design.

Looking Ahead. The next chapter, Your Best Is Ahead of You, explores how to embrace this momentum and push beyond perceived limits. Growth is not static; it is a continuous process of becoming. As you take control of your journey, remember: your best is not behind you; it is still ahead, waiting to be discovered.

SOMETHING TO PONDER

Unsuccessful people make decisions on their **current situation**. Successful people make decisions based on where they **want to be**.

Call to Action: This is a good time to reflect and to take note of your thoughts.

1. **Commit to Reflection**. Set aside time each day to write down one win, one lesson, and one thing you must improve. Stick to it. It is your path to growth.

2. **Know Your Worth**. List three things you are good at or proud of, skills, traits, or achievements. Keep this list visible and add to it weekly.

3. **Define Greatness**. Ask yourself, "What makes me feel proud versus just okay?" Write one step to turn a 'good' effort into a 'great' one this week.

TAKE THE NEXT STEP IN YOUR JOURNEY

Your journey of growth is not a destination. It is an ongoing, ever-evolving loop of **learning, self-reflection and continuous improvement**. The next step is to take full ownership of your progress by developing a **structured self-reflection positive habit** that will keep you moving forward.

This exercise is not just about reviewing where you have been, it is about **actively shaping where you are going**. The clarity you gain will empower you to celebrate achievements, recognize opportunities for improvement, and maintain a growth mindset.

Before moving on to the next chapter, commit to **owning your journey**. Every day is a new opportunity to move from good to great.

TURNING TOWARD THE LIGHT: REFLECTIONS FOR GROWTH

Reflection 3 – **The Power of Choice**

Every day, you make choices; some so small they seem inconsequential, others so significant they shape the trajectory of your life. Yet, behind each choice lies a story: a motivation, a hesitation, or a belief. Was it fear that guided you? Convenience? Or was it a deep alignment with the values and goals that truly matter to you?

Choices are powerful because they define who you are and who you can become. Imagine standing at a crossroads, where one path feels safe and familiar, while the other is uncertain but full of potential. The direction you choose in that moment says more about your aspirations than anything else.

When guided by intention, even the smallest decisions become stepping-stones toward fulfilment. Choosing courage over comfort, growth over stagnation, and values over convenience transforms your life into a reflection of your best self.

Reflection: Examine your choices, and ask: Are my decisions leading me closer to the life I want?

Call to Action: Stop, take a few minutes and reflect upon the following:

- **Reflect on Your Choices**. Think of a decision you made recently. Write down what guided it: fear, convenience, or alignment with your values.
- **Plan Your Next Step**. Identify one upcoming decision, big or small. Ask yourself, which choice aligns with the person you to become. Commit to acting on that decision.
- **Choose Growth**. Take one bold action this week that pushes you beyond your comfort zone. Let this choice reflect courage, intention, and your future aspirations.

11

YOUR BEST IS AHEAD OF YOU

As you embark on the next step of your journey, one truth becomes clear: your best is always ahead of you. The path of self-improvement is not a destination but an ongoing evolution, a testament to the wisdom we gain through reflection, and the revelations that shape our growth. While it is not my intent to impose faith or beliefs on anyone, I firmly believe that wisdom and revelation are blessings, gifts that illuminate the distinction between experience and understanding, between knowledge and true insight.

Growth is a lifelong journey. It is not about perfection but progress, celebrating the small, daily wins that build momentum toward long-term transformation. It requires leaving behind the limiting beliefs of the past, embracing the opportunities that lie ahead, and recognizing that your best self is not a fixed point. With each intentional action, you step closer to a more fulfilled, capable, and resilient version of yourself.

This chapter is an invitation to reflect, realign, and reignite your pursuit of the best version of you. It is a reminder that no matter where you stand today, the journey forward holds infinite potential for growth, achievement, and purpose. Let's explore how to keep moving toward the best that lies ahead.

Wisdom vs. Experience. Experience is the accumulation of events, actions, and decisions that shape our journey through life. It is what we live, see, and feel, a personal catalogue of successes, failures, and the moments in between. However, experience alone is not transformative. Wisdom, by contrast, is the ability to extract meaningful lessons, discern patterns, and apply understanding derived from those experiences to make sound decisions. Where experience is the teacher, wisdom is the mastery of what is taught.

Wisdom transcends mere experience because it demands reflection, humility, and the openness to learn not only from our own lives but also from others. It equips us to look ahead, leveraging the past without being bound by it. Wisdom transforms experience into purposeful action, guiding us toward growth and greater fulfilment.

Revelation vs. Knowledge. Knowledge is the accumulation of facts, skills, and information that we learn through study, observation and practice. Revelation, however, is a deeper moment of clarity, insight, or understanding that often surpasses the boundaries of knowledge. Revelations challenge us to see beyond the surface, connect to something greater, and uncover meaning that logic or data alone might overlook.

Revelations act as catalysts, unlocking doors that knowledge alone cannot open. They spark innovation, ignite purpose, and illuminate pathways that may have been obscured. Where knowledge builds the framework, revelation breathes life into it, inspiring us to think differently, act courageously, and align more fully with our purpose.

Why Your Best Is Ahead of You: While experience and knowledge are valuable, they are merely the raw materials for becoming your best self. Wisdom and revelations are what shape and refine them, turning potential into reality. To reach your best self, you must actively pursue these gifts through reflection, intentional growth, and an open mind that is willing to embrace new perspectives.

Your best version lies ahead because you are constantly evolving. Every challenge and triumph, every moment of reflection, adds to the foundation from which wisdom is built. Each insight, whether gained through study or a sudden revelation, draws you closer to a life of greater clarity, purpose, and fulfilment.

Growth is not linear, nor is it confined to what you know today. The gap between where you are and where you want to be is bridged by your ability to transform experience into wisdom and knowledge into revelation. The truth is that your best self is not a fixed point; it is a horizon, a moving target defined by your willingness to grow, adapt, and thrive.

As you step forward, remember: your best is yet to come. This is not an empty promise, but a reality rooted in the nature of growth and possibility. Whether you are navigating life's twists or reflecting on your journey so far, the story of your life is still unfolding, and the best chapters are ahead.

I was a below-average student in school. I had convinced myself that my circumstances at home gave me a free pass to adopt an "I do not care about school" attitude. And when I embraced that mindset, no one seemed to challenge it. I thought I was winning because no one nagged or interfered. In my youthful arrogance, I believed I had outsmarted everyone, managing to slip under the radar so I could do as I pleased.

At 18, I got my first job as a delivery driver. Picture this: a young man driving a double-wheeler van through the narrow streets of Malta's beautiful three cities found in the south of our beautiful island. The van was packed to the brim with goods and, on one memorable day, I was delivering several heavy products to a local store. With no available parking, I had to stop in the middle of the road, blocking traffic, including a Waste Collection Truck, the local waste truck. The truck's driver, waiting impatiently, eventually leaned out and in very vulgar words yelled at me, "Hey you, are you moving anytime soon?" (these words are the polite version).

I was mortified. His words cut through me, leaving me overwhelmed with embarrassment. At that moment, I felt a deep sense of regret and self-reproach. My "I do not care" card had led me to this point, a version of myself I could not bear to see. I realized that staying in that version would lead me nowhere. Something had to change.

That day was a turning point. I resolved to grow, to evolve. I turned to education, finding an interest in information technology that sparked my curiosity. At the time, my aspirations were modest: I simply wanted to transition from being 'that boy' to someone with a fulfilling career. I never imagined myself as a CEO or an entrepreneur; I just wanted to belong somewhere, to feel pride in my work, and to create opportunities for myself.

I began setting goals and dedicating myself to personal and professional growth. Along the way, life presented challenges that tested me, personally and professionally. There were moments of joy and triumph, but also tears, anger, and doubt. Despite it all, one thing remained constant: my commitment to structured self-reflection, my commitment to Thrive On.

I attribute much of my success to this process of introspection. It helped me stay grounded, measure my progress and constantly strive for improvement. Over the years, I have identified

> five principles that guided my journey, and I highlight one now: structured self-reflection.
>
> I urge you to embrace yourself fully: your flaws, your strengths, and your potential. Love yourself enough to seek growth. Do not settle for 'good' when greatness is within reach. Your best version is not a distant dream; it is ahead of you, waiting to be uncovered through discipline, reflection, and the unwavering belief that transformation is possible.

From Crossroads to Creation. Life continually presents us with crossroads, pivotal moments where choices shape who we are becoming. The transition from adolescence to adulthood is often the first of these defining moments, as the safety of childhood gives way to the responsibilities of independence. Education, work, and relationships each bring decisions that influence our path.

But the true power lies not just in the choices themselves, but in how we prepare for them. Education, whether formal, vocational, or self-taught, equips us with tools. Experience then refines those tools, turning them into mastery. When you actively seek knowledge, hone your skills, and deepen self-awareness, you evolve from a mere participant in life to the architect of your journey. You do not merely choose a path; you create it.

The Myth of Luck and the Truth of Preparation. It is easy to attribute success or fulfilment to luck, yet this perspective diminishes the effort behind achievement. Luck is not an accident; it is the meeting point of preparation and opportunity.

Consider this: even if you hold a lottery ticket, would you stake your future on it? Success, unlike a gamble, is built on deliberate preparation, persistence, and purpose.

The truth is simple: those who succeed consistently invest in themselves. They sharpen their skills, embrace challenges, and position themselves to seize opportunities. This is not luck; it is strategy, and it is a strategy available to anyone willing to take action.

The Power of Believing in the Next Step. Believing that your best is ahead is more than optimism; it is transformative. This belief shifts your focus from the past to the future, from what has been to what can be. It redefines challenges as opportunities and inspires you to take ownership of your growth.

Picture the best version of yourself. What habits, skills, and attitudes does this version embody? Now ask, "What is one thing I can do today to move closer to that vision?" The distance between who you are and who you wish to become is bridged by small, consistent steps.

Anchoring Growth in Reflection. Structured self-reflection is a cornerstone of growth. Each day offers lessons, but it is through deliberate reflection on your achievements, setbacks, and areas for improvement that you build a cycle of continuous progress. With each reflection, you align your actions more closely with your goals, creating momentum toward becoming your best self.

Beyond the Comfort Zone. Your comfort zone, while offering safety, is also a silent thief. It steals potential, dulls curiosity and invites complacency. Growth resides on the other side of discomfort, in the moments that test your resilience and challenge your boundaries.

The journey beyond comfort is not about reckless leaps but intentional, courageous steps. Whether it is acquiring a new skill, embracing constructive feedback, or confronting a fear, each deliberate action expands the edges of your comfort zone. Over time, challenges that once seemed insurmountable will become the foundation of your strength.

A Mindset of Continuous Growth. The belief that your best is ahead fosters resilience, possibility, and action. With structured self-reflection, you realize that, no matter your age or past experiences, your most fulfilling achievements and joyous moments still await. Growth becomes a journey of progress, not perfection, marked by small wins and transformative insights.

Embracing Challenges as Opportunities. Consider a challenge you are currently facing. Instead of viewing it as an obstacle, shift your perspective to see it as an opportunity to grow. This mindset transforms setbacks into stepping-stones, turning every difficulty into a chance to evolve into a stronger, wiser version of yourself.

A Journey Without End. Your best version is not a final destination but an ongoing pursuit. Each step forward unveils new horizons and fresh opportunities for growth. This journey is uniquely yours, a testament to your resilience, self-awareness, and commitment to continual evolution.

Commit to this mindset today: your best is always ahead. Set meaningful goals, reflect deeply and embrace each challenge with confidence. The mirror does not lie; it reflects not just who you are, but who you are becoming. Look into it, see your potential, and take the next step forward.

Transition to Invest in Yourself. As you embrace the mindset that your best self is ahead, you will discover that the journey requires deliberate action and strategic investment. Growth is not accidental; it is intentional. The next chapter, Invest in Yourself, will guide you through the practices and principles of making that investment into your skills, your wellbeing, and your future. By dedicating time, energy, and resources to your own development, you lay the groundwork for a life of purpose, fulfilment, and impact.

SOMETHING TO PONDER

"World-class begins where the comfort zones end" is a rule the successful, the influential, and the happiest always remember.

Call to Action: This is a good time to reflect and to take note of your thoughts.

1. **Own Your Future**: Write down one reason why your best days are not behind you. Repeat it to yourself every morning this week.

2. **Move from Stuck to Start**: Think about one decision you have been hesitating on. Take the first step today, whether it is sending a message, asking a question, or planning your next move.

3. **Trust the Process**: Write one small step you can take toward your goal today, no matter how simple. Believe that this step has the power to create momentum.

TAKE THE NEXT STEP IN YOUR JOURNEY

To truly embrace the belief that **your best version is ahead of you**, you must shift your mindset from thinking of success as a destination to recognizing it as an **ongoing journey of growth and transformation**. The next step is to **visualize your future self, define the habits and qualities you need to develop, and take intentional action toward becoming that person**.

This exercise is not just about dreaming of a better version of yourself, it is about **creating a clear road map to becoming that person**. The insights you gain will empower you to adopt the right mindset, take meaningful steps, and continually strive for improvement.

Before moving on to the next chapter, commit to **believing in your future and taking action today**. Your best version is not behind you. It is ahead, waiting for you to step into it.

TURNING TOWARD THE LIGHT: REFLECTIONS FOR GROWTH

Reflection 4 – **Your Inner Dialogue**

Your inner voice is always speaking. Sometimes it whispers encouragement, cheering you on when you need it most. Other times, it is a harsh critic, planting seeds of doubt and insecurity. This dialogue shapes how you see yourself, your choices, and your future. The words you say to yourself, positive or negative, carry immense power.

Imagine walking through life with a constant companion. If that companion were uplifting and supportive, you would feel confident and inspired to take on the world. But if they were critical and harsh, you would doubt every step. The truth is, your inner voice is that companion, and it is with you every moment of your journey.

The good news? You have the power to rewrite that dialogue. By choosing to nurture a kinder, more compassionate inner voice, you can turn it into your greatest ally.

Reflection: Listen closely to what your inner voice is saying and begin transforming it into a source of encouragement and growth.

Call to Action: Stop, take a few minutes and reflect upon the following:

- **Listen to Yourself**. Write down one common thought your inner voice says to you, positive or negative. What is its impact on you?
- **Rewrite the Script**. If negative, take that thought and transform it into an encouraging statement. Say it to yourself daily this week, especially when self-doubt arises. What are you going to say to yourself?
- **Create a Habit of Kindness**. Each night, write down one kind thing you did for yourself or others. Let this habit shape a more compassionate inner dialogue.

12

INVEST IN YOURSELF

The best version of you is always ahead, but reaching it requires one undeniable truth: you must invest in yourself. Imagine a world where you are your greatest asset, a resource so powerful that every moment spent nurturing, refining, and empowering it yields infinite returns. This is not a distant fantasy; it is a reality within your grasp only if you choose it.

Yet, too often, we devote our energy to jobs, relationships, and obligations, leaving little for the one person who matters most: the one steering the ship, you. Neglecting to invest in yourself is not just a missed opportunity; it is a choice to limit your growth and dim the possibilities that await. Without this intentional effort, the goals you have set, the Thriveon principles you have adopted, and the vision you hold for your best self will remain unfulfilled.

Investing in yourself is not selfish, it is vital. It is the foundation for every success, every breakthrough, and every meaningful contribution you will make. In this chapter, we will delve into why this investment is the cornerstone of personal growth, what it truly entails, how to begin the journey, and when to prioritize it. Because, without this commitment, every strategy, reflection, or ambition becomes futile.

If your best is ahead of you, the path forward begins here: by making yourself the greatest priority.

THE "WHY": WHY INVESTING IN YOURSELF MATTERS

- **The Foundation for Growth**. You are the core of everything you do. Your wellbeing, mindset, and skills directly influence how you perform in life, connect in relationships, and contribute to the world. By investing in yourself, you strengthen this foundation, enabling better decision-making, resilience in the face of challenges, and the capacity to excel.

- **The ROI (Return on Investment)**. Investments in yourself have the highest returns. Whether it is learning a new skill, improving your health, or fostering emotional intelligence, every step you take toward personal development pays dividends. A publication by LinkedIn[9] stresses the importance of investing in oneself and how this can lead to greater career opportunities, higher earning potential and, above all, increased job satisfaction.

- **The Consequences of Neglect**. Failure to invest in yourself leads to stagnation. According to a Gallup survey, only 23% of employees are actively engaged in their work, often because they feel underdeveloped.[10] This disengagement is not limited to jobs; it seeps into personal lives, affecting relationships, mental health, and overall satisfaction. Investing in yourself prevents this plateau and ignites ongoing growth.

- **Taking Ownership of Your Growth and Happiness.** The findings from Gallup's State of the Global Workplace Report paints a sobering picture: only 10% of workers in the UK are engaged in their roles, with the majority struggling both at work and in life. Globally, employee engagement stagnates at 23%, while stress and negative emotions permeate the workforce. These figures are a stark reminder that waiting for external factors, such as better leadership, improved workplace policies, or new opportunities to drive your personal development is a risky gamble.

To thrive in today's challenging landscape, you must reject the expectation that others, whether employers, mentors, or society, will shoulder the responsibility for your personal growth and fulfilment. Real change begins with you. It is up to you to own your journey, act and lead by example.

If you desire mentorship, coaching, or support from others, the first step is to demonstrate that you care about your own development. Walk the talk. Show up for yourself by committing to the Thriveon Method outlined in this book. The effort you invest in defining your goals, tracking your progress, and addressing areas for improvement will not only elevate your own life but also inspire those around you. People are far more willing to support and invest in someone who is already taking meaningful steps toward their growth.

Personal fulfilment is not granted; it is earned. By taking ownership of your development, you build credibility, resilience, and self-respect. These qualities set a foundation for long-term success, irrespective of external circumstances. Start now. As this book emphasizes, your best self is waiting just beyond your comfort zone.

THE "WHAT": WHAT TO INVEST

- **Time**. Time is your most valuable currency. Yet, research shows that most people spend more time on social media or watching TV than on self-improvement. Dedicating even 20 to 30 minutes a day to personal growth can transform your trajectory.

- **Honesty and Commitment**. Personal investment requires brutal honesty. Acknowledge where you need improvement, whether it is in discipline, health, or skills. Combine this awareness with commitment and the resolve to make consistent efforts.

- **A Positive Attitude**. Growth thrives on positivity. A can-do mindset allows you to embrace challenges as opportunities rather than obstacles. Focus on progress over perfection and celebrate small victories along the way.

- **Resources**. Invest in books, courses, mentors, and tools that align with your goals. For instance, if you are pursuing physical fitness, a good pair of running shoes and a fitness tracker could be game changers. If it is knowledge, a library card or a subscription to an online learning platform might be your starting point.

- **Discipline**. Consistency is the bridge between goals and results. Discipline ensures you show up even when motivation wanes. It is the daily ritual that compounds into meaningful change.

THE "HOW": THE PATH TO PERSONAL INVESTMENT

The process of self-investment is not at all complex, but it requires structure and commitment. These are concise guidelines:

Reflect Regularly. Using tools like the Thriveon Method's structured self-reflection, daily reflect by asking these four questions in relation to your defined goals (destination) and PSMs (signposts):

- Today / Yesterday what did I achieve?
- Today / Yesterday what did I learn?
- Today / Yesterday what could I have done better?
- What MUST I change?

Set SMART Goals. To effectively answer the Thriveon questions, you must first set your destination. Where are you? Where do you want to get to in the next week, month, year? Articulate your goals and ensure that these are Specific, Measurable, Achievable, Realistic, and Time-bound.

Leverage PSMs (Personal Success Metrics). Decompose your goals to measurable PSMs. Define metrics for success in areas like physical health, professional growth, and personal development. For example:

- Physical health PSMs: Walk 10,000 steps a day.
- Personal development PSMs: Read for 20 minutes daily.

Track Your Progress. Use journals, apps, or even a simple notebook to monitor your performance and growth. With commitment, daily iterate through the Thriveon questions.

Celebrate Wins. Acknowledge progress, however small, to build momentum and self-confidence.

THE "WHEN": MAKING TIME FOR YOU

The best investment in yourself comes with a routine. Set aside 20 to 30 minutes, five days a week, for reflection and growth. This positive habit ensures consistency while allowing flexibility for weekends, holidays, and breaks.

Morning Routine: Reflecting on "Yesterday"

Dedicate time between 5 am and 9 am to look back on the previous day. This quiet window allows you to analyse what worked, what did not, and how to improve. Morning reflection sets the tone for the day, energizing you with purpose and clarity.

Evening Routine: Reflecting on "Today"

If mornings do not suit you, carve out time between 5 pm and 8 pm to reflect on the day that just passed. This practice helps you close the day with intention, clearing your mind and preparing for the next day.

The Flexibility of Timing

There is no one-size-fits-all approach. The key is consistency. Choose a time that aligns with your schedule and stick to it, treating it as a non-negotiable appointment with yourself.

Real-Life Inspiration: The Power of Self-Investment

Consider Warren Buffett, who famously spends 80% of his day reading and thinking.[11] This commitment to self-investment has made him one of the most successful investors in history. Or think of Oprah Winfrey, who dedicates time to meditation and reflection daily, crediting these habits for her resilience and creativity.[12]

You do not have to be a billionaire or a celebrity to reap the rewards of self-investment. A single mother learning coding online to transition into tech or a retiree taking up painting to nurture creativity are equally powerful examples of how self-investment transforms lives.

> Investing in yourself is the single best investment you can make. Growing up in one of the smallest villages in Malta during the early 1980s, acquiring a computer was no small feat.

At the time, purchasing one required not only months of waiting but also declaring your intent to government authorities. After much anticipation, I finally managed to secure a small computer, a Commodore 64.

By today's standards, where even the simplest smartphone far surpasses the capabilities of that computer, the Commodore 64 might seem laughably outdated. However, for me, it was a portal to a new world of learning and possibilities.

I am sure many young people today would find this situation hard to imagine, or perhaps not understand it at all, through no fault of their own. My Commodore 64 was connected to a small, 15-inch black-and-white television using a coaxial cable, the same communication protocol used to link televisions to outdoor aerials that dominated Malta's skyline at the time. When I turned the computer on, nothing happened except for a blinking cursor in the top-left corner of the TV screen. The machine looked lifeless.

Thank goodness for the manual. Opening it for the first time, I was introduced to the BASIC programming language. The manual explained various reserved words (commands) and offered examples of how they could be combined to create activity on this seemingly inert machine.

I quickly realized that if I wanted to make this computer come alive, I needed to invest in myself.

I had to dedicate time. I had to prioritize being at home over being with my friends. I had to choose learning over playing games on my computer. It required my full heart and mind engagement to learn how to develop software, and it was clear that this path was the way forward for me.

The more I immersed myself, learning became fun. I began envisioning conceptual models and relished the challenge of transforming those concepts into digital reality. My first accomplishment was writing a routine to display multiplication tables on my screen (or rather, my TV). From there, I learned how to capture user inputs, store data on cassette tapes, and much more. I had learned how to celebrate small wins.

Looking back, that period of my life was one of the best investments I have ever made. Not only did it lay a solid foundation for my career, but it also helped me discover a new version of myself, a version full of curiosity, ambition, and the belief that I could shape my own future.

Make Yourself a Priority. Investing in yourself is a commitment that extends beyond skills and achievements; it is the foundation for a fulfilled and purposeful life. By prioritizing personal development, dedicating time to habits that nurture growth, and ensuring self-care, you create a wellspring of energy and resilience. Remember, each deliberate step you take today builds the foundation for your future self. This is not a fleeting task but a lifelong journey of progress.

As you prepare to envision the person you aspire to become, let this chapter serve as a reminder that every effort you invest in yourself is a seed planted for tomorrow's harvest. The journey of personal investment paves the way to clarity, strength, and impact.

From here, let us move forward into defining and refining that vision of the person you must aspire to be. In the next chapter, The You, You Must Aspire To, we delve deeper into shaping your future self, grounded in emotional intelligence, actionable goals, and an unwavering belief in the power of growth.

Your best self awaits you.

SOMETHING TO PONDER

When investing in your self-image and self-worth, the place to start is from self-belief. Yes, you can.

Call to Action: This is a good time to reflect and to take note of your thoughts.

1. **Choose Positivity**: Start each morning by listing three things you are grateful for. Write them down or say them out loud.

2. **Make Yourself First**: Block out one hour this week just for you. Use it to learn, relax, or work on a personal goal.

3. **Celebrate You**: Pick one recent win, no matter how small, and treat yourself, whether to a favourite snack, a walk, or sharing your success with someone close.

TAKE THE NEXT STEP IN YOUR JOURNEY

To truly embrace the power of **investing in yourself**, you must shift your mindset from viewing personal growth as an afterthought to making it a **deliberate and ongoing priority**. The next step is to **identify key areas of self-investment, create a plan for continuous improvement, and commit to taking action every day**.

This exercise is not just about setting goals. It is about **making a long-term commitment to your personal growth and wellbeing**. The clarity you gain will empower you to take small, intentional actions that lead to **lasting change and success**.

Before moving on to the next chapter, commit to **investing in yourself daily**. Your future self is counting on you.

13

THE YOU, YOU MUST ASPIRE TO

The journey to becoming the best version of yourself is a profound investment in your growth, potential, and future. As we explored in the previous chapter, investing in yourself is the cornerstone of achieving your aspirations. Without this essential foundation, dreams risk fading into disappointments and frustrations. To aspire to a new you, you must not simply hope for change. You must commit to deliberate actions that makes transformation possible. Only through sustained personal investment can aspirations evolve into realities.

This chapter, The You, You Must Aspire To, invites you to envision and shape the person you are destined to become. It is a journey that demands self-discovery, deliberate action, and a steadfast commitment to improvement. Thriveon's philosophy centres on this transformative process, guiding individuals beyond the confines of their comfort zones into a realm of continuous growth. Here, we explore the profound elements of emotional intelligence, the transformative power of mindset and the decisive shift from inertia to initiative, offering a vision of the person you can become.

The Role of Emotional Intelligence. At the heart of this transformation lies emotional intelligence (EI), the cornerstone of both personal fulfilment and professional success. While intellectual abilities may open doors, it is emotional intelligence that ensures you thrive in relationships, careers and life's unpredictable challenges. To understand EI is to unlock the ability to manage emotions, your own, and those of others effectively and empathetically.

Self-Awareness. The Foundation of EI. Self-awareness forms the bedrock of emotional intelligence. It is the ability to recognize and understand your emotions as they arise, reflect on what drives your behaviours, and align your actions with your core values. This awareness is not innate; it must be cultivated through intentional practices like journaling, mindfulness, and self-reflection. Pausing to examine your thoughts and reflect on your day provides clarity, illuminating the path to growth and better decision-making.

Emotional Regulation. The Art of Mastery. Equally vital is the ability to regulate emotions, especially when they threaten to overpower rational thought. Emotional regulation is not about suppressing feelings but channeling them productively. It enables you to stay composed under pressure, navigate conflicts with grace, and maintain focus when faced with adversity. Mastery of this skill is a hallmark of emotionally intelligent individuals who turn emotional energy into positive action.

Empathy. The Bridge to Connection. Empathy is the ability to step into another's shoes and truly understand their joys, struggles, and perspectives that transforms relationships into powerful alliances. Empathy builds bridges between people, fostering connection, collaboration, and trust. It enables you to respond with compassion and insight, creating bonds that elevate both personal and professional relationships.

Self-Motivation and Social Skill. Keys to Progress: emotional intelligence also demands self-motivation and social adeptness. Self-motivation drives you to pursue goals not out of obligation but with purpose and passion. It ignites the inner fire that fuels resilience and perseverance. Social skill, on the other hand, ensures these aspirations are communicated effectively, fostering collaboration, trust, and teamwork. Together, these qualities lay the foundation for growth, adaptability, and sustained success.

This chapter challenges you to embrace emotional intelligence as a guiding force in your journey. With each step, you draw closer to becoming the person you aspire to be: one who thrives not only in achievements but in relationships, purpose, and fulfilment.

> The journey to becoming the person you aspire to be begins with a clear vision, actionable goals, and unwavering commitment. In my younger years, I was deeply involved with an organization focused on delivering information technology training courses. My role was in business development and sales and, together with my colleagues, we built a reputable training force in Malta. At the time, it was rare to find certified trainers and materials in specialized areas like project management, systems analysis and design, and software development. To address this gap, we collaborated with trainers from the UK,

establishing a mutually beneficial arrangement to deliver high-quality training in Malta.

One of our scheduled courses was PRINCE2, a demanding ten day project management training program that was fully booked. It was during this course that I met Donal McGranaghan, an Irishman and gentle giant, who had traveled to Malta to deliver the training. Watching Donal in action was inspiring, not just because of his technical expertise, but because of his ability to connect with his audience. He had a unique way of making each participant feel seen and valued, fostering an atmosphere of respect and collaboration. His emotional intelligence was palpable in the way he encouraged questions, provided constructive feedback, and adapted his teaching style to meet the group's needs.

In our conversations, when he learned about my background and IT involvement, he suggested I join him in Dublin as a contractor for a company specializing in banking systems to take on a role in systems analysis, design, and software development. Initially, I thought Donal was simply being kind. But his belief in me ignited something within, a desire to improve, to grow and to change my circumstances. Donal became more than just a trainer; he became my mentor, helping me chart a course toward the person I aspired to be.

Donal's belief in my potential was not blind optimism; it was grounded in his ability to read people's strengths and inspire confidence. His emotional intelligence as a coach was evident in how he recognized my hesitations and countered them with encouragement rooted in practical advice. He once said, "Growth is earned, not granted." This resonated deeply with me and became a guiding principle in my journey.

With his guidance, I set clear goals and PSMs, backed by a strong will to climb higher and achieve more. Soon after, I had a phone interview with Donal's employer in Dublin and was offered a three-month contract, with the possibility of extensions based on performance. This opportunity not only brought financial stability but also began restoring my self-confidence and respect, which had wavered due to personal challenges I was facing at the time.

I approached this opportunity with a clear plan. I immediately asked about the criteria for extending my contract beyond the initial three months. Once I understood what was expected of me, I translated those requirements into specific PSMs and used the Thriveon Method for daily self-reflection. By consistently measuring my progress and staying disciplined, I ensured I was prepared for the renewal meeting.

In this process, I leaned heavily on emotional intelligence. I knew that technical skills alone would not guarantee success. Building trust with my colleagues required empathy, active listening, and humility. I sought help openly when I did not know something, ensuring that I met the team's expectations without pretension. This approach fostered trust, respect, and collaboration, creating a foundation for success. When the day came, I successfully secured a six-month extension.

While in Dublin, I professionally thrived but faced emotional struggles. My family was back in Malta, and this was before the age of mobile phones, video calls, or frequent flights. I missed my family deeply and wanted to be closer to home. With this in mind, I set a new strategic goal: to secure a contracting opportunity in London, which would allow me to commute weekly and spend weekends with my loved ones.

Now I had two clear goals:

1. **Tactical Goal**: Ensure contract renewals in Dublin.

2. **Strategic Goal**: Secure a role in London for better work-life balance.

To achieve these, I established separate PSMs. For the tactical goal, I focused on delivering exceptional results in my current role. For the strategic goal, I created PSMs around personal development (acquiring new skills), networking (connecting with industry professionals in London), job searching, and refining my CV.

Through disciplined adherence to the Thriveon Method, with daily self-reflection and a positive attitude, I systematically worked toward both goals. Every interaction in Dublin became an opportunity to practice EI, whether it was empathizing with colleagues' challenges, maintaining a positive attitude despite homesickness, or showing resilience during setbacks.

After my second six-month renewal in Dublin, I also achieved my strategic objective: I was offered a subcontractor role at Heathrow Airport with a major airline as an Agile Consultant. This move allowed me to strike a better balance between work and family, spending weekdays working in London and weekends at home in Malta.

Both goals were achieved because of deliberate planning, consistent effort, and a commitment to growth. Donal's mentorship taught me that, while academic intelligence can secure a job, emotional intelligence builds a career.

> By cultivating trust, respect, and care, I not only achieved my goals but also became a better version of myself. His belief in me helped me believe in myself, and that belief became the foundation for everything I achieved thereafter.

Your mindset is the lens through which you view yourself and the world. It has the power to shape your destiny. Those with a fixed mindset often perceive their talents and abilities as static, avoiding challenges out of fear of failure, and seeking validation from others. By contrast, a growth mindset thrives on the belief that abilities can be cultivated through effort, learning, and persistence. It sees challenges as opportunities to evolve and embraces failure not as an endpoint but as a stepping-stone toward success.

The transformation from a fixed mindset to a growth mindset begins with how you reframe challenges. Where a fixed mindset sees obstacles as insurmountable, a growth-oriented perspective uncovers possibilities waiting to be explored. This shift is not instantaneous but, with deliberate effort and consistent self-reflection, the growth mindset can become your guiding principle. You begin to focus not solely on the outcomes but on the journey itself, valuing the effort it takes to achieve meaningful goals. Each small victory along the way reinforces your belief in the possibility of growth, making the process as rewarding as the destination.

A growth mindset also nurtures resilience, the ability to navigate setbacks with determination and strength. By celebrating progress, even in its smallest forms, you develop the courage to persist through uncertainty and doubt. Growth requires embracing the discomfort of challenges, knowing that every effort moves you closer to your aspirations.

At the same time, inertia, the force that keeps us stuck in routines that no longer serve us, becomes a significant barrier. Often fueled by fear, whether of failure, change, or the unknown, inertia creates an illusion of safety while quietly stifling your growth. Breaking free from this cycle is an act of reclaiming agency over your life. It means stepping boldly into action, taking ownership of your decisions, and embracing the uncertainty of change.

The antidote to inertia is initiative, the ability to act with intention and without waiting for external prompts. Initiative requires identifying opportunities, setting clear goals, and taking deliberate steps forward. It is not about rushing but about moving forward with clarity and purpose. Reflection becomes an indispensable part of this process, allowing you to evaluate your progress, learn from missteps, and adjust your course as needed. In this way, initiative is not merely about doing more; it is about doing what truly matters.

Aspiring to become the best version of yourself is one of life's most profound commitments. The person you must aspire to be is not an unattainable ideal but an authentic reflection of your deepest values, resilience, and purpose.

You must align daily actions with long-term goals, guided by emotional intelligence, a growth mindset, and proactive initiative. You must navigate relationships with empathy, embrace challenges as pathways to growth, and take purposeful steps toward their dreams.

This version of you does not resist change but welcomes it as a catalyst for progress. You celebrate every step forward, no matter how small, and use reflection to continuously learn, adapt, and improve.

By committing to this journey, you inspire others, not through perfection, but through your unwavering dedication to becoming better each day.

The journey to becoming your best self is lifelong. It is shaped by intentional choices, disciplined actions, and meaningful reflections. When you embrace emotional intelligence, foster a growth mindset, and act with initiative, you unlock the tools to live a life that is not only successful but deeply fulfilling. The person you aspire to be is not an impossibility, it is the result of the actions you take today.

Your best self is always ahead of you. But the true goal is not just to pursue personal greatness; it is to align your aspirations with a life of purpose, contributing meaningfully to all segments of your life.

Begin this journey now, and witness how your life is "A Life Worth Living."

SOMETHING TO PONDER

Believe before you see. Focus on the imagery of your new self, and before you know it, you will meet your new self.

Call to Action: This is a good time to reflect and take note of your thoughts.

1. **Know Your EQ**: Reflect on how you handle stress, feedback and relationships. Ask yourself, how well do I understand and manage my emotions?

2. **Grow Your EQ**: Choose one small action to improve today, like pausing before reacting, actively listening, or expressing gratitude.

3. **Separate Big from Small**: Write one long-term goal (strategic) and one short-term step (tactical) to get closer to it. Focus on balancing both.

TAKE THE NEXT STEP IN YOUR JOURNEY

To truly embrace **the you, you aspire to**, you must shift your mindset from simply wishing for a better version of yourself to actively **building and becoming that person**. The next step is to **define your aspirational self, identify the habits and beliefs that will shape your growth and take daily actions that bring you closer to your full potential**.

This exercise is not just about imagining who you want to be, it is about **aligning your mindset, habits, and actions with your highest potential**. The clarity you gain will empower you to move forward with **purpose, confidence, and intentionality**.

Before moving on to the closing chapter, commit to **stepping into the person you are meant to be**. Your best version is not behind you It is ahead, waiting for you to claim it.

14

CONCLUSION: A LIFE WORTH LIVING

Every journey worth taking eventually circles back to a single, powerful question: *was it worth it?* Not in the currency of fame, money, or fleeting applause, but in the quiet, personal moments when you meet your own reflection and feel at peace with what you see. This final chapter is not a summary, nor a goodbye. It is a call to continue. A reminder that the real rewards in life are earned through the invisible work. The internal battles, the small daily choices, the courage to keep growing when no one is watching. This is about more than achievement. It is about crafting a life of meaning, resilience and fulfilment. One that, when you look back, feels not only lived but truly worthwhile.

Embracing Lifelong Growth. To live a life worth living, you must continuously strive to grow, learn, and push beyond your limitations. Many people let their intellectual curiosity die young, surrendering to routines and abandoning self-improvement. But personal growth is about staying intellectually and emotionally alive throughout your life.

Avoid your intellectual death and cultivate a mindset of lifelong learning. No matter your age or past experiences, personal growth is available to you. Embracing a life worth living means committing to continuous improvement, fostering resilience, and understanding that your best self is always evolving. This is the foundation of a fulfilling life.

The Courage to Keep Growing. It takes courage to look in the mirror and see both your potential and your areas for growth. Encourage yourself to embrace this journey with optimism and a willingness to change. The process of self-improvement can be challenging but, with your own conscious leading, you have the support needed to face these challenges and grow from them.

Building a Legacy of Growth. Living a life worth living is not just about personal success; it is about building a legacy of growth, resilience, and self-discovery. By investing in yourself, pushing beyond your comfort zones and embracing the mindset that "your best is yet to come," you set an example for others and inspire them to pursue their own journeys.

The Essence of True Fulfilment. At the heart of this book lies one unshakable truth: life's greatest treasures are not measured in possessions or accolades, but in the depth of love, respect, and trust we cultivate, first within ourselves and then with others. Success is not about bank accounts or grand achievements. Success is fulfilment, the profound satisfaction that comes from living authentically, growing continuously, and nurturing meaningful relationships.

The purpose of this final chapter, and indeed this entire book, is to remind you of life's true riches and to provide a road map for achieving them. The goal is not to amass wealth but to cultivate a life of purpose and fulfilment. This journey begins with you. To love, respect, and trust yourself is to unlock your ability to offer the same to others, creating a foundation for a life rich in connection, joy, and meaning.

LESSON 1: IF YOU ARE GOING TO FAIL, FAIL FAST

Failure is not the enemy. It is a teacher, a momentary guide showing us the boundaries of our current understanding. When we shy away from failure, we deny ourselves the lessons that come from trying, adjusting, and growing. The key is to fail fast: do not linger in the discomfort or dwell on mistakes longer than necessary. Instead, analyse, learn, and move forward. Growth is born in these moments of courage and reflection.

In my own journey, I failed more times than I can count. Some failures stung deeply, others embarrassed me, and a few felt insurmountable at the time. But every single one of them taught me something. These lessons became the stepping stones toward success, not obstacles. When you embrace failure as part of the process, you learn to adapt quickly, iterate relentlessly, and move closer to your goals with each attempt.

LESSON 2: IF YOU FAIL TO PREPARE, YOU ARE PREPARING TO FAIL

Preparation is the backbone of achievement. Success does not come from chance or luck; it is built through deliberate effort, planning, and execution. To live a life worth living, you must know what you are striving for. Define your goals and prepare for the challenges ahead.

When I was working to transform my life from a delivery boy to a professional in IT, preparation became my shield against uncertainty. Whether it was studying late into the night, setting specific milestones, or reflecting daily on my progress, every moment of preparation laid the foundation for my future success.

Ask yourself: *"Am I prepared for future challenges?"* Are you equipping yourself with the tools, knowledge and mindset needed to thrive? If not, now is the time to start.

LESSON 3: THE CHASE OF ONESELF IS FAR MORE INTERESTING THAN THE FINDING OF ONESELF

Many people talk about "finding" themselves, as if identity is a static treasure waiting to be uncovered. But life is not about finding, it is about becoming. It is about the chase, the pursuit of your evolving self. Who you are today is not who you will be tomorrow, and that is a beautiful thing. Embrace the process of transformation and enjoy the journey of discovering what you are capable of.

For years, I chased stability, success, and knowledge, but what I ultimately found was the joy of the pursuit itself. Each step forward revealed a new layer of who I could be. The process of chasing my better self became the most fulfilling part of my life. The chase is what keeps me curious, motivated, and alive.

LESSON 4: BE EMPOWERABLE, FOR WITH EMPOWERMENT COMES ACCOUNTABILITY

Empowerment is not something bestowed upon you; it is something you must be open to receiving. To be empowerable means to take ownership of your choices, actions, and growth. True empowerment does not come without accountability. When you accept responsibility for your life, you gain the power to shape it.

In my life, empowerment began when I stopped blaming circumstances and started owning my decisions. No longer could I point to external factors as excuses. Instead, I learned to reflect deeply, set clear goals, and hold myself accountable to achieving them. When you take ownership of your life, you unlock the potential for real change.

FULFILMENT: THE TRUE MEASURE OF SUCCESS

Love, respect, and trust: these are the core ingredients of a fulfilling life. When you cultivate them within yourself, you create the foundation for deep, meaningful relationships with others. This harmony between self and others is where happiness is born. It is the essence of what makes life worth living.

When we chase material possessions or external validation, we are filling a void that cannot be satisfied by such means. True fulfilment comes from within. It comes from knowing that you have lived with integrity, grown with intention, and nurtured relationships that matter. It comes from looking in the mirror and seeing someone you are proud to be.

> Life is undeniably worth living. It is a tapestry woven with moments of joy, discovery, and resilience. Traveling and immersing yourself in what lies beyond your everyday norm opens doors to perspectives you never imagined, enriching your soul in ways words often cannot capture. Friendships form another vital thread, those shared laughs, the fond memories of carefree moments, and the deep conversations that leave lasting imprints on your heart.
>
> Life's worth is also revealed in its challenges. I have faced hurdles that seemed insurmountable, situations where all hope appeared lost. Yet, time and perseverance often unveiled outcomes I could never have anticipated, transformations that reminded me of the strength and possibility within us all.

> And then, there is family. To know the meaning of unconditional love, to experience its warmth in the comfort of those who stand by you no matter what, that is a gift that amplifies life's value. These moments of connection, triumph, and love are the essence of what makes life not just worth living, but extraordinary.

Your Final Reflection. As you close this book, take a moment to pause and reflect. What does a life worth living truly look like to you? What deliberate steps will you take to pursue the best version of yourself? Remember, the mirror never lies, it reflects your truth. When you gaze into it, ask yourself: *"Am I living authentically?" "Am I embracing growth?" "Are my actions aligned with my purpose?"* If the answer is no, take heart, for your best self is not behind you, it is still ahead of you, waiting to be claimed.

A life worth living is not shaped by monumental moments alone but by the sum of small, intentional choices made every day. It is built through self-respect, love, and unwavering trust in yourself and others. It is a life rich with joy, driven by purpose, and deepened by genuine connections. It is a life where growth becomes your legacy, a gift you pass on not only to yourself but to those whose lives you touch.

So, now, the journey continues. Go forth with courage, clarity, and conviction. Seek the best version of yourself and, in doing so, inspire others to do the same. Create a life that is not only meaningful to you but leaves an indelible mark on the world.

That is the life worth living.

The mirror is waiting, and your reflection is ready to evolve.

I wish you nothing less than the very best.

15

ABOUT THE AUTHOR

IVAN was born in September 1965 on the island of Malta, an isolated yet culturally rich nation nestled in the heart of the Mediterranean Sea. While Malta's size has remained constant at just 316 square kilometers, at the time its population was under 400,000, and its economy was sustained largely by tourism and modest manufacturing.

He is the youngest of three siblings, growing up in a small village where community ties were tight, and privacy was scarce. It was a place where everyone knew everyone and everything about them. In such an environment, character was not optional; it was a prerequisite for survival.

His sister, the eldest, was compelled by their father to marry her fiancé before the couple emigrated, a decision rooted in the traditional values of the era. His brother, six years his senior, married young and relocated to Scotland. By the age of 12, Ivan was effectively home alone. With both parents working, he was forced to become independent early, learning that survival began with self-reliance.

At school, Ivan was an average student with little prospect of university. External circumstances and internal doubts created detours that he accepted, albeit for all the wrong reasons. Still, deep within, a spark retained an ember of faith that refused to extinguish.

At 18, he entered the workforce as a delivery man, navigating Malta's winding roads in a van that doubled as his first classroom. There, he learned the fundamentals of resilience and adaptability. He realized he was heading nowhere fast and that transformation had to begin with him.

A turning point came when he stumbled across an article titled "Measure Your Own Performance." It introduced him to the After-Action Review, a tool used by the military to evaluate performance. This was his epiphany. Structured self-reflection became his method of navigating life's complexities and remains a central pillar of his philosophy.

In the early 1980s, information technology in Malta was still embryonic. When Ivan acquired his first computer, a Commodore 64, he was instantly hooked. His fascination was so intense that his mother, alarmed, called the parish priest for guidance, believing something was seriously wrong. She could not have been more mistaken. Ivan had found his calling.

By the age of 20, he was a self-taught software developer. A year later, he became self-employed, with only a brief period of traditional employment from 1991 to 1996. During that time, he worked across government and the private sector, gaining invaluable insights and hands-on experience. He also enhanced his academic profile in information technology, attending specialized courses in the United Kingdom certified by the British Computer Society. These engagements expanded his knowledge base and opened doors to collaborate with experts from the UK, Canada, the USA, and South Africa. These relationships cultivated his understanding of leadership, innovation, and collaboration.

In 2001, at age 36, Ivan founded 6PM, an IT company which started as a solo venture but quickly scaled. By 2007, the company was listed on the Malta Stock Exchange, becoming the nation's leading software house. At its peak, 6PM employed over 200 professionals and operated out of Malta, England, Ireland, and Macedonia. Among his proudest achievements were winning a European Award for Innovation, receiving Malta's Entrepreneur of the Year award, and becoming the first Maltese individual to be honoured with a Doctor of University Honoris Causa from Middlesex University.

6PM's healthcare software went on to serve clients such as the UK's National Health Service, establishing its reputation in the sector. In 2017, the company was acquired by a publicly listed firm on the London Stock Exchange. Ivan officially closed this chapter in February 2018.

From a boy growing up in a village with limited opportunity, to a man who built and exited a multinational tech enterprise, Ivan's life is a testament to the power of reflection, grit, and the belief that one's future is not dictated by their beginnings. He did not let the physical limitations of his island define him. Over the decades, his work has taken him across the United Kingdom, North America, Scandinavia, and Europe, broadening not just his business footprint but his worldview.

Today, Ivan is committed to sharing the method that shaped his success. Chief among them is a structured approach to self-reflection, a tool he credits as transformative. Alongside this, his unwavering faith in God has remained a steadfast light through both triumph and adversity.

ENDNOTES

1. "An evening With Dua Lipa (Live from the Royal Albert Hall) (CBS Full Version)" video uploaded on www.youtube.com on 2024-12-23 https://youtu.be/1O0BbFhJXil?si=f7bJ3gddbWLlQ9Gl

2. "Library of Congress Blogs; posted on 29 July, 2024 – https://blogs.loc.gov/inside_adams/2024/07/frederick-winslow-taylor-scientific-management/

3. "The Druker Institute – Claremont Graduate University; last modified 6 June, 2023"; https://drucker.institute/about-peter-drucker/

4. "Harvard Business Review; first published in the *Harvard Business Review* January – February 1992 edition. https://hbr.org/1992/01/the-balanced-scorecard-measures-that-drive-performance-2

5. Science Direct – Pareto Principle https://www.sciencedirect.com/topics/computer-science/pareto-principle

6. Poetry Foundation; The Poems of Emily Dickinson Edited by R. W. Franklin (Harvard University Press, 1999) https://www.poetryfoundation.org/poems/52202/forever-is-composed-of-nows-690

7. George Barna, "Millennials Establish Their Need for Purpose and Lifestyle Changes," Cultural Research Centre at Arizona Christian University, 9 November, 2021. - https://www.arizonachristian.edu/wp-content/uploads/2021/11/CRC_Millennial_Report01_Digital_01_20211109.pdf

8. Simply Psychology, Maslow's Hierarchy of Needs, by Saul McLeod, PhD, updated on 14 March 2025. https://www.simplypsychology.org/maslow.html

9. "The value of investing in skills in this modern era; published 1 July 2024". https://www.linkedin.com/pulse/value-investing-skills-modern-era-likemindrecruitment-zbfwe/

10. "Global employee engagement stagnates while wellbeing declines" by Rob Moss; published 12 June 2024". https://www.personneltoday.com/hr/gallup-state-of-the-workplace-2024-employee-engagement-wellbeing/

11. Buffet Online cached by LiteSpeed Cache on 16 April 2025. https://buffett.online/

12. From The Oprah Magazine published in August 2016. https://www.oprah.com/inspiration/what-oprah-knows-about-the-power-of-meditation